HAL LINDSEY

and
Biblical
Prophecy

HAL LINDSEY

and Biblical Prophecy

C. Vanderwaal

PAIDEIA PRESS
St. Catharines, Ontario, Canada

Table of Contents

Preface

On a trip to Canada in 1974, I visited St. Catharines (near Niagara Falls), where I got involved in a discussion with a preacher (the Rev. Raymond J. Sikkema of Trinity Christian Reformed Church) and a businessman who had started a publishing company (John Hultink of Paideia Press). In the course of our conversations, I was given a copy of Hal Lindsey's book *The Late Great Planet Earth*. A request was made of me: Would I be willing to read carefully through this book, which had made such an impression on evangelicals in North America? Could I perhaps write something about Hal Lindsey and his approach to Biblical prophecy? That request I accepted as an assignment.

Reading *The Late Great Planet Earth* convinced me that Hal Lindsey is a spokesman for a movement with a tremendous impact on the Christian public. I then went on to study some other publications of the same sort and became acquainted with the source from which they had sprung—Darbyist dispensationalism.

As a result, I felt called to write about Lindsey's views. Yet it did not seem wise to write about Lindsey alone, for another Hal Lindsey might soon rise to prominence and supplant him, presenting essentially the same dispensationalist viewpoint in a popular, engaging style. A book devoted solely to this rising star would not be quite as useful as one that also dealt with the background of his thought and the source of his ideas. Early in the book, therefore, I will deal with dispensationalism.

7

Now, I want it to be clear from the outset that I am not interested in unleashing a heresy hunt. Hal Lindsey is clearly on fire for the gospel. For this we commend him. Moreover, he is an appealing figure in his own way. All the same, we cannot avoid confronting the urgent question what position to take with regard to the new dispensationalism—the dispensationalism that Lindsey defends in such a clear and popular style.

When Hal Lindsey appeared on television in the Netherlands, it became clear that even sober Calvinists welcomed his dispensationalism with open arms. His predictions about the future were accepted and believed. Clearly the Christians there were defenseless when confronted with his misleading ideas. One Dutch preacher observed sadly:

> I shudder when I think of all the faithful church members who have lost their way because of Hal Lindsey. What disturbs me especially is not the book as such—although it is shockingly naive in theological respects—but the fact that so many people who should know better fall for it hook, line and sinker. Whenever I attend a gathering of preachers, I find them expressing amazement at the fact that church members who have grown up on Reformed preaching and catechism instruction are taken in by such literature—and even have the gall to say that they are now being confronted with the Biblical message for the first time.

Naturally, I could not help wondering just how this phenomenon is to be accounted for. My effort to answer this question forced me to deal with certain views on the book of Revelation and the "end time" that are in vogue today. It became apparent to me that many dispensationalist motifs have crept into Reformed thought bit by bit. Moreover, I could easily point out frameworks of thought, distinctions, and models that have paved the way for the dispensationalist outlook. Because of its affinity with such patterns of thought, dispensationalism did not have a hard time forcing its way into the Reformed camp.

It should come as no surprise that the question of the proper interpretation of the last book of the Bible plays a major role in my evaluation of dispensationalism. A mistaken understanding of the book of Revelation leaves the door wide open to dispensationalism.

I have been encouraged by Mr. Hultink to lay down some main lines with regard to the interpretation of the Revelation to John. I would like to thank him—together with Rev. Sikkema—for stimulating me and helping me along.

Scores of pious Christians are simply infatuated with Hal Lindsey. If that scares us—and it certainly should— couldn't we best respond by taking a fresh look at the book of Revelation and the issues that arise from our interpretation of it?

Since the 1930s, the last book of the Bible has been my chief scholarly preoccupation. I dealt with it in my doctoral dissertation, and later I wrote an extensive commentary on it. Over the years I have become more and more convinced that our interpretation of this book is trapped in a blind alley. Why? Because we fail to ask ourselves how God's covenant with His people ties in with the New Testament.

What role does the covenant play in our thinking? Is it simply forgotten once Christ appears on the scene as the fulfillment of the Old Testament prophecies? My hope and plea is that this question will again be taken seriously in our time, now that we face the Hal Lindsey phenomenon.

It's not enough, of course, to point out what's wrong with Cocceian or dispensationalist or Kuyperian views of the covenant. Our understanding of the covenant must come to fruition in our interpretation of Scripture. It makes no sense to combat a certain view of the covenant and then accept readings of Scripture based on the view we have just rejected.

I am firmly convinced that the covenant's relevance to the reading of the New Testament needs emphasis in this age of television and the *Reader's Digest*. Saving a few souls from the dispensationalist flood will do little good if we fail to turn off the dispensationalist tap. (The same is true of Pietism, Methodism, existentialism, and sensationalism, of course.)

The book of Revelation is not an ugly duckling out of place among the other books of the New Testament. No, Revelation is itself a covenantal book through and through. Only when we realize this and think out the consequences will we be in a position to determine just where dispensationalism goes wrong. Let no one be so foolish as to think that the dispensationalist tide can be stemmed by means of an outlook on Scripture that springs from the same family as Hal Lindsey's views. Such a defense will not hold back the dispensationalist tide for long.

What was my purpose in writing? To appeal to my fellow believers to uphold the Reformed confession in more than name—to uphold it by accepting its consequences for the interpretation of Scripture.

Apocalyptic Themes in Our Culture

Apocalypse

The strange word *apocalypse* is derived from the name of the last book in the Bible. In Greek this book is called the "Apocalupsis" of John, i.e. the "Revelation" to John.

We are so accustomed to calling this book the Revelation of *John* that we forget that it is really the Revelation of *Jesus Christ.* John is only the *receiver* of the revelation—not its source. Strictly speaking, it is Christ's Revelation *to* John.

It is widely assumed that the book of revelation deals with future events. Since John's "Apocalypse" makes use of symbols and figurative language, it has become customary to speak of any writing that uses mysterious language and deals with "the last things" as "apocalyptic."

This regrettable development has emptied John's "Apocalypse" of its meaning for many people. The books we so often speak of as "apocalyptic" are not revelations of God and Jesus Christ. In fact, most of them breathe a spirit that is the very opposite of the gospel.

What does the word *apocalyptic*, which has become so popular in our time, really mean? According to the *Penguin English Dictionary*, it means "of or like the Apocalypse; prophetic of vast disasters; like the end of the world."

The word *apocalypse* has become a catchall. We speak of Jewish apocalypses, such as IV Ezra, the book of Enoch, and the Jewish Sibylline Books. We also speak of early

11

Christian apocalypses, such as the Shepherd of Hermes and the Apocalypse of Peter.

We apply this word to medieval writings as well. Dante's *Divine Comedy* is often characterized as "apocalyptic." We speak of apocalyptic elements in the writings of the mystics and the Anabaptists. Even Communism is sometimes called "apocalyptic"—because of its eschatology. What major religion or ideology has not been accused of harboring apocalyptic elements?

The uncertainty prevalent in the world today, now that the international order is so unstable, drives people to look for something to hang on to. "Prophecy"—another word that is often torn from its Biblical context and turned into a general cultural phenomenon—will have to save us. Some people anxiously read horoscopes; others turn to Jeanne Dixon for light on the future. Books are written about the collapse of the West, the collective suicide of the industrialized world, the Great Machine, the twenty-first century, the year 2000, and the Hour beyond the Final Hour. Eagerly we discuss "apocalyptic" authors like Orwell, Aldous Huxley, and Gheorghiu.

The fear of atomic warfare refuses to go away. The incredible technological advances made in our time have brought about a growth and intensification on all levels. The rapid increase in scientific knowledge has led to a corresponding increase in evil and misery. Where will our Operation Superman lead? To an antichrist?

The forces of evil seem to be winning. When the United Nations was founded, people pointed out that the prospect of the world coming to an end was being taken seriously for the first time in many centuries. Hence all the interest in "apocalyptic" writings and the use of such terms as *bowls of wrath, dies irae,* and *Armageddon* in recent literature.

There is a twentieth-century version of the Apocalypse. The traditional terms are used—but they are given a new content, sometimes a nihilistic, extremely pessimistic content. The widespread interest in the paintings of Hieronymous Bosch is revealing.

When it comes to "apocalyptic" material, there's something for everyone. Children are fascinated by the prospect of invaders from outer space. Full-size children (i.e. adults who have never grown up) likewise devour science fiction, which even manages to work in "religious" apocalyptic themes nowadays. And futurology has been elevated to the rank of a science.

Journalists were quick to realize that apocalyptic themes catch the attention of the public. If people are shown a threat to their existence, they listen. Moreover, entertainers discovered that the people of our time just can't seem to get enough when it comes to stories (true or false) dealing with fear and disasters. Regular doses of apocalyptic terror are demanded by the public. People actually seem to enjoy the apocalyptic land of terror and the unknown.

Apparently there is a deep-seated love of the gruesome in many of us. Do you remember how circuses used to make money by displaying freaks for the public to gawk at? In the freak shows put on by today's journalists and entertainers, there are many revolting sights to be seen. You can even get the scare of your life in a *Biblical* setting!

Apocalyptic themes are big business for journalists and producers of mass entertainment. A public that reads nothing heavier than the *Reader's Digest* is ready to consume and digest great quantities of the terror treatment.

Christians are also guilty of cashing in on the "apocalyptic" boom. The Christian journalists with apocalyptic wares for sale will be our special concern in this book. (Remember that I'm talking about *pseudo*-apocalypses, the non-Biblical speculation about the future that we find in so many Christian periodicals and books.)

The "Christian" boom in books on doom

Throughout the centuries there have always been "journalists" who produced "Christian" apocalyptic writings. Today they are becoming too numerous to count. As we get closer and closer to the ominous year 2000, their numbers keep increasing.

Isn't the interest in "apocalyptic" themes universal in our time? Well then, some Christians argue, here's a role for us. We're the ones who should point the way. After all, we have the Bible. And the Bible reveals the future, doesn't it? Thus *we* can outline the future, quoting chapter and verse. The political events are neatly laid out for us. All we have to do is wait for the prophecies to be fulfilled. Fortunately, we already have certain indications that the battle lines are being drawn up. Think of the Arab-Israeli conflict, the role Russia now plays in the Middle East, and so forth.

In a foreword to *The Coming Russian Invasion of Israel,* a book by Thomas G. McCall and Zola Levitt, Hal Lindsey writes: "I feel this book is a must for everyone who wants to know where we are on God's time-table." The need of the hour, then, is to discover what point we have reached in God's great travel plan.

There are plenty of futurologists in today's pulpits. For them the Bible is not just a travel guide in the sense that it sends the comfort and admonition of the Word of God along with us on our path through life. No, Scripture includes much more for them. It gives us—or them, at least—God's timetable, His overall plan, His task for the nations of our time. It's all laid out in the Bible—literally and in detail. If you want to know about the coming invasion of Israel by the Russians, read Ezekiel 38 and 39.

Many people who have long been immersed in "worldly" apocalyptic literature are now turning eagerly to the "Christian" brand that is being shoved under their noses. The exaggeration and sensationalism is just what appeals to them. As a result, there is a steady stream of such "Christian" apocalyptic literature rolling off the presses—especially in North America.

Thus we have good reason to take a careful look at this phenomenon. And there's another factor to consider. These journalistic tactics pave the way for a dangerous error, an error that undermines the work of the church, our evangelism programs—indeed, all our Christian endeavors. That error is *dispensationalism.*

Revolutionary tendencies in "Christian" apocalyptic literature

Before we focus our attention on dispensationalism itself, I must point out another important facet of today's "Christian" apocalyptic literature—the revolutionary element. Why does such literature fit in so well with our rebellious age? Precisely because of the revolutionary tendencies it contains!

When Spiro Agnew was Vice President of the United States, he listed what he called the "ten commandments of the protester," to describe how protesters actually operate. Three of them were: Don't give your opponent a chance to respond. Don't concern yourself with the lessons of history. Don't write anything longer than a slogan.

The apocalyptic journalists with their revolutionary tendencies operate in the very same way. They forget about history. History has no support to offer them anyway. Thus the history of exegesis doesn't concern them in the slightest. All they're interested in is "the latest"—especially if it's startling or sensational. The problems with which theologians have wrestled for centuries are quickly forgotten.

These journalists are so interested in the future that their back is turned to the past and its lessons. And they don't make proper use of the work of contemporary theologians either. (They quote them only when it's to their advantage.) Their stock in trade is human fear and man's interest in the gruesome.

Apparently the public finds this immature self-confidence exciting. These journalists make no attempt to refute earlier interpretations of the Bible passages on which everything is made to depend. The views of past scholars are simply shaken off as dead weight. It all seems so clear and obvious that there's nothing left to question or argue about. One can't help being reminded of the sales pitch of the Jehovah's Witnesses, for that's just the kind of acceptance of dubious interpretations that these journalists hope to wring from the Christian public.

We must learn to recognize the *revolutionary* streak in this development. The democratization of our society has now gone so far that *anyone* can be an authority on Biblical interpretation. Do it, brother! Don't let anyone stand in your way!

The dogma of evolution is part of this revolutionary outlook. On the strength of some "law of development," people are told that our own century is more important than any of the many centuries that preceded it. Aren't the predictions of the prophets being fulfilled in *our* time?

People like to hear such flattering language. "We're living in electrifying days of fulfillment of ancient Biblical prophecies," says Hal Lindsey. Within the current dispensation, our own age is a very special time, he tells us. Then he hauls out a few texts that seem to fit such a time-scheme. He can't miss!

We live in a time when church life is declining and many preachers are willing to try almost anything in an effort to win back an audience. But the erosion continues. Such a time is ripe for an outlook that ignores the past and glorifies the present. Sad to say, even Christian writers cash in on this lamentable situation. The result is that the spiritual descendants of Luther and Calvin succumb to a hermeneutical anarchy adorned with Bible texts.

Because revolution in turn seeks to create new institutional forms, we should not be surprised to see dispensationalism produce a catechism of its own. Wim Malgo, who has something in common with both Hal Lindsey (he was once a sailor) and Abraham Kuyper (he was born in the Dutch town of Maassluis), appears on the scene with his *Fifty Questions Most Frequently Asked about the Second Coming.* In this book he breaks completely with the Heidelberg Catechism's teachings about the covenant.

To see this for yourself, however, you must be well acquainted with what the Heidelberg Catechism teaches, for Malgo does not come right out and contradict it. Neither does he take issue with the Reformed position on the covenant in any other direct way. He simply ignores it. As a result, Reformed believers who do not know the Reformed confessions as well as they should are taken in. They assume that Malgo comes along in these "electrifying days" to *supplement* what the church already confesses, or that he is presenting something that the church has long kept hidden in some archive.

The fact of the matter is that Malgo's catechism casts aside the teaching of the Reformers. It's a case of revolution in disguise. Like other revolutions, it has no time for history, for its self-confidence is unassailable. To top it off, this revolution comes packaged in a best seller. It's presented in such a way that the "thinking man"—the age of rationalism is far from over—gets the impression that he is personally involved in the discovery of these new truths, which are dug up in the Bible, of all places!

But what does Scripture itself say? Is interpreting Biblical prophecy as plain and simple as Hal Lindsey would have us believe?

The Dispensationalist Error

Using Biblical prophecy to foretell the future

The disciples were not the only ones who asked Jesus when He would restore the kingdom of Israel. Throughout the ages there have been many who dared to take it upon themselves to reveal the secrets of the future on the basis of Biblical prophecy. Horrible events just around the corner have been foretold repeatedly by self-styled prophets who declared that the end was near, that Christ was about to return.

One such prophet was Montanus, who lived in Asia Minor in the second century. Two prophetesses supported him in his prophecy, which led to the rise of what we might call a charismatic movement. Montanus believed that he was the bearer of the Holy Spirit, the Paraclete. In him the prophecy of John 14:16-18 had been fulfilled. Via displays of ecstasy and tongue-speaking, he declared that the New Jerusalem would descend to earth at Pepuza to inaugurate the millennium.

Apparently Montanus did not realize that John 14:16-19 and 16:13-14 had already been fulfilled: the Lord's revelation to the apostles was already recorded in the New Testament Scriptures. Montanus believed in a continuing revelation—or rather, in a revelation that attained its completion in his own "prophecy." Thus he went far beyond what was written.

His highhanded interpretation led him to *localize*

18

Christ's coming. *When* would Christ return? Montanus declared that it would happen soon and called for an adventist attitude. *Where* would Christ return? The New Jerusalem would descend to earth at Pepuza.

The "prophecy" of Montanus represents a model that we see again and again in church history, in all sorts of variations. Biblical prophecies are made the springboard for prophecies based on one's own supposedly charismatic heart and mind.

In other early Christian writings, such as those of Irenaeus and Hippolytus, we also come across calculations of when and where Christ will return. Most of these calculations were based on the books of Daniel and Revelation. Fortunately, such speculations were only peripheral phenomena in the life of the church. In later sectarian movements, however, they assumed a much more central place. Yet, the writings of the church fathers are not above reproach on this score either.

In the middle ages we encounter the figure of Joachim of Fiore, who lived from about 1130 to 1202. Proceeding from the doctrine of the trinity, Joachim divided history into three periods. The Old Testament era was the period of the Father, a time of the letter, of the flesh, of the law. Then came the age of the Son; in that age was born a church that conformed largely to the world. The age of the Son comes between the letter and the spirit. The third age is the time of the Holy Spirit, a time in which spiritual monks will bring the eternal gospel (Rev. 14:6). This third, spiritual period was to begin around the year 1260, according to Joachim. (Think of the 1260 days mentioned in Revelation 12:6.)

In the year 1210, Francis of Assisi (1182-1226) was given permission by the Pope to organize a new religious order. The dominant wing of this new order made use of the ideas of Joachim to present itself as the vanguard of a new spiritual day that was dawning.

Here we see spiritualism and apocalypticism going hand in hand, with the books of Daniel and Revelation again providing the necessary Scriptural data. Within this spiritualist circle there arose speculation about the seven ages of the church. We shall see that this idea of the church's seven ages has remained alive to this very day.

In the time of the Reformation, mystics and Anabaptists were especially receptive to apocalyptic thinking à la Joachim. Again we see a charismatic movement going hand in hand with a revolutionary movement both intensely interested in the "last days," which have already arrived or are just around the corner. All of this contributed to the drama in Münster in 1535.

The prelude to this drama was the appearance on the scene of Melchior Hofmann, a furrier. Hofmann let it be known that he was one of the two witnesses of Revelation 11, namely, Elijah. Seven years after the appearance of the two witnesses, the millennial kingdom would be inaugurated at Strasbourg. Under the leadership of Hofmann, the 144,000 would then preach the gospel throughout the entire world.

As you read the rest of this book, don't forget that Hofmann already spoke of a seven-year period. Where did he get that figure? In Revelation 11:2 we read about 42 months, and in the very next verse about 1260 days. Add them together, and you get seven years. (The mistake in this procedure is that the same period of time is being referred to in the two verses.)

Hofmann was arrested in Strasbourg in 1533. Ten years later he died in prison there. In the meantime, a baker named Jan Matthys appeared on the Anabaptist stage. Before long he was hailed as the other witness of Revelation 11—Enoch. On the basis of revelations from heaven, this apocalyptic figure declared that the Lord had rejected Strasbourg as the new Zion and had chosen Münster (in Westphalia) instead. When Christ returned, He would appear in Münster. Thus the geographic locale shifted through Matthys.

Matthys sent twelve apostles throughout the Netherlands to get everything ready. The Anabaptists even succeeded in seizing control of Münster. After Jan Matthys died in a skirmish, John of Leiden took over and became king of the heavenly Zion. As you may know, this episode ended in a complete fiasco.

It's striking that the proponents of the theology of liberation are so interested in the apocalyptic literature of the Anabaptists and mystics. Do they recognize themselves in those figures of long ago?

The fall of Münster as the new Zion in 1535 did not put an end to the adventist way of thinking. Even in well-established Protestant churches, speculation about the future was rife. Pietism, which was rapidly gaining ground, often went hand in hand with a belief that the millennial kingdom would soon dawn and that the Jews would be converted in droves.

Among Reformed Christians, the doctrine of the seven ages of the church came into fashion through Cocceius (1603-69), who picked up themes espoused by the Franciscan spiritualists. Cocceius was a professor at Franeker and later at Leiden. He was the leading figure in the Netherlands in the theological battles of his own time and even beyond his time.

The interesting thing about Cocceius is that we find an element of dispensationalism in his thought. He made the doctrine of the covenant central, but he did not accept the continuity of the covenants. The new covenant completely superseded the old one because it had a different content.

For the rest, I could make quite a number of positive comments about this great scholar, who deserves to be remembered for his famous Hebrew dictionary alone. Important for our purposes is that his disciples stressed his more dubious doctrines, such as his theory of the seven ages of the church.

Johann Albrecht Bengel (1687-1752) is often called the father of Pietism. On the basis of various calculations, he decided that Babylon's dominance would begin in 1810, and that the beast of Revelation 13 would make its appearance in 1832. As for the millennial kingdom, it would begin on June 18, 1836.

The famous scientist Isaac Newton (1642-1727) had already figured before him that the year 1715 would be the beginning of the end. Later he changed his prediction to 1766.

The mention of Newton brings us into the Anglo-Saxon world. America also played a role in this eschatological speculation. In fact, the charismatic movement flourished especially in America, thanks to the "frontier mentality." The various revivals created a climate in which apocalyptic seeds of all sorts found fertile soil.

William Miller (1782-1849) decided that Christ would return on March 21, 1843. He based his conclusion on Numbers 14:34—"for every day a year." Using this text as his key, he translated the 2300 days of Daniel 8:14 into years. Assume that Jerusalem was rebuilt in 457 B.C. and start counting. The magic year is 1843. When Christ did not appear on schedule, Miller and his followers moved the date back, just as the Jehovah's Witnesses changed their date when their prophecies about the year 1975 failed to come true.

But such disappointments did not put an end to the expectations and calculations of the adventists. In reaction to the coldly Modernistic rejection of Christ's return in favor of a way of thinking that recognizes only horizontal relationships, Fundamentalists and sectarians have persisted in building up far-fetched eschatological systems. As long as the leaders and self-styled prophets claimed to be filled with the Holy Spirit, they were not bothered with criticism and troublesome questions.

Protected by the charismatic shield, even amateurs could construct novel, exciting apocalypses. In the face of the insecurity and rudderlessness of modern man, they offered something concrete and positive, something to hang on to—something supposedly drawn from the Bible, at that!

Many people who clearly want nothing to do with the life of the church are still receptive to an appeal to the Bible and are even willing to base their way of life on a few loose texts pulled from here and there. During the Reformation era, the Anabaptists provided comfort to the "laity" and the "poor in spirit" (whom the Catholic hierarchy had deliberately kept in the dark) by filling them with apocalyptic ideas. In our time it's not much different; the apocalyptic Gnostics of the nineteenth and twentieth centuries play the same game. The tragedy is that those who have lost their way reach out eagerly to such "prophets."

Love of the sensational also plays a role here, of course. Moreover, let's not forget the revolutionary mentality of both the leaders and the led, which manifests itself in their refusal to pay any attention to history or tradition. This mentality leaves the door open to a charismatic radicalism, which then proceeds to preach its bizarre vision of the future.

Dispensationalism

John Nelson Darby (1800-82) was an Irishman who became a preacher in the Anglican Church. Gradually his eyes were opened to the shortcomings of the established church with its privileges. As a result, he broke with the Anglican Church in 1828, but he didn't stop there. He also broke with the very idea of the church as an institution. Only free gatherings of believers were acceptable to him. No office-bearers were needed.

His followers were known as "Darbyists." They were also called "Plymouth Brethren," for in the English town of Plymouth Darby had come across a circle of believers whom he regarded as a model to be copied everywhere.

Darby wanted nothing to do with a fixed confession. Here again we see a contempt for history—the same revolutionary attitude that we already encountered in other sectarian circles.

When Darby broke with the Biblical idea of the church, he also rejected the doctrine of the *unity* of the covenants. He divided redemptive history into dispensations or segments. In each dispensation we see God working with humanity in a *different* way. This is necessary because of the changes in mankind as it grows from childhood to maturity.

Each dispensation fails before the shift to the next one is made. And in each dispensation God makes different demands on man. In the Mosaic dispensation, the demand is obedience to the law of Moses. In the Christian dispensation (in which we live), the demand is acceptance of the gospel through faith. There is little continuity between one dispensation and the next. In Darby we find elements reminiscent of Cocceius.

As for the future, Darby taught that the believers will be taken up to heaven when Christ returns the first time (without being seen). That return will bring the dispensation of the church on earth to an end. But it will not mean the end of history! The Old Testament dispensation will then be restored.

Darby proceeded from the thesis: "Prophecy is prewritten history" (*Collected Writings*, II, p. 217). In their explanations of the covenant in force after the Rapture, the Darbyists talked of a seven-year period (think of Melchior Hofmann). During this period, 144,000 Jews will be converted and will undertake a massive evangelism campaign (Melchior Hofmann again). At the same time, the Roman empire will be restored. Then the Great Tribulation will begin, only to end at Armageddon.

In this context we find the Darbyists speculating about Russia, which is destined to play a major role at the end of time. Meshech is Moscow, Rosh is Russia, Tubal is Tobolsk, and so forth (Ezek. 38).

After Armageddon Christ will come to earth for the second time—visibly. All the saints who were taken up to heaven will return with Him. That event will inaugurate the millennial kingdom, which in turn will end at the time of the last judgment.

Darby visited the United States and Canada a number of times, and his influence went far beyond the circles of the

Brethren. His dispensationalist teaching found acceptance among Christians of various denominations who wanted to be orthodox. By now dispensationalism is firmly planted in the territory it has carved out for itself among Christians of the type usually referred to as "Fundamentalists" or "evangelicals."

In 1909, the famous *Scofield Reference Bible* appeared. (A revised edition was published in 1967.) This Bible advanced the cause by pushing the dispensationalist viewpoint in the notes. Many believers deeply committed to the Scriptures accepted this study Bible as an orthodox reference work and thereby came to accept a popularized version of dispensationalism.

The word *Fundamentalism* is derived from a series of publications entitled *The Fundamentals: A Testimony of Truth.* This series, which began in 1909, sought to defend the basic principles of the Christian faith in the face of the onslaught of Modernism, which was rapidly gaining ground in the United States.

Because Fundamentalism clung so stubbornly to certain doctrines without taking the whole of Biblical revelation into proper account, the movement went wrong. As a skeletal, fragmentary confession, it was in no position to keep out simplistic thinking and spiritualism. The movement also proved to be lacking in intellectual integrity. Moreover, it was open to eccentric influences of all kinds. Because it neglected the ties between the present and the past and was often shockingly lacking in theological awareness, Fundamentalism gave birth to a climate in which Chiliastic and dispensationalist ideas could easily creep in and be absorbed.

As the dispensationalist system was built up, expectations about Israel played an ever larger role. The founding of the state of Israel and the subsequent political events in the middle east became "proofs" of the dispensationalist apocalypse.

Although earlier dispensationalists were inclined to apply the facts about Israel to the millennial kingdom, the emphasis now falls more on the seven-year period after the "church" is "taken up." In this period after the Rapture, the antichrist will make a covenant with Israel. Moreover, the temple will be rebuilt and the Great Tribulation will begin—after 3 1/2 years have gone by.

Such an outlook reduces the gospel message to a warning to be prepared for Christ's sudden, invisible return. If you miss out on the Rapture, you will be subjected to the torments of the second half of the seven-year period! The dispensationalist appeal to conversion, which has a distinct Arminian flavor, is then backed up with a description of the horrors of the coming world war.

Dispensationalism and the covenant

Dispensationalism emphasizes the different dispensations in redemptive history. In itself this is not wrong, for Scripture does talk about various dispensations and covenants between man and God. But when the dispensationalists proceed to work out the details, they destroy the unity of administration of the covenant of grace.

Seven dispensations are distinguished and then given the following distinct characterizations:

Dispensation	Characteristic
Paradise	Innocence
Adam	Conscience
Noah	Human control
Abraham	Promise
Moses	Law
Christ	Grace
Millennium	Kingship

These dispensations differ from each other in structure. Although the Christian dispensation is characterized by faith and grace, there are some dispensationalists who find room for faith and grace in the Mosaic dispensation—but without making grace central.

Dallas Theological Seminary is a stronghold of dispensationalist thinking. Its "Doctrinal Statement" affirms:

> We believe that three of these dispensations or rules of life are the subject of extended revelations in the Scripture, viz. the dispensation of the Mosaic law, the present dispensation of grace, and the future dispensation of the millennial kingdom. We believe that these are distinct and are not to be intermingled or confused, as they are chronologically successive.

From this it follows clearly that the Old Testament dispensation is at best a covenant of works and not a covenant of grace. My question is: Aren't the Old Testament covenant and the New Testament covenant really two parts of one and the same covenant of grace?

Scripture is very clear on this point. There are indeed different dispensations, but there is only *one* covenant, and it always has the same structure. The character of this covenant can be summed up in the words *promise, command,* and *threat.* In the different dispensations, the covenant remains one in structure, for the God of promise, command and threat remains the same.

Throughout church history, the unity of the covenant has often been doubted and attacked. It was Marcion who began the tradition of contrasting the Old Testament God, as the world's vengeful Creator, with the God of love presented in the New Testament. Among the Gnostics we see a similar development. The Anabaptists also pulled the two covenants apart; as a result, they lost sight of the value of the Old Testament.

The Reformers, however, maintained that Jesus' renewal of the covenant did not lead to a covenant with an entirely different structure. All that changed was the manner in which the covenant was administered. Calvin observed:

> The covenant made with all the patriarchs is so much like
> ours in substance and reality that the two are actually one
> and the same . . . . Christ the Lord promises to his followers
> today no other "Kingdom of Heaven" than that in which
> they may "sit at table with Abraham, Isaac, and Jacob" (*Institutes of the Christian Religion*, 2.10.2 and 23).

Because the covenant is one, we may never await a different sort of covenant in which kingship rather than grace is central, a covenant that allows people another opportunity to repent and be converted after the time of the covenant of grace has passed. The current dispensation of the covenant is basically no different than the Old Testament dispensation. The *current* covenant, that is, God's way of dealing with man in the past and the present, is determinative for the future.

Dispensationalism must stand or fall with its view of the covenant. There are people who take a dim view of the disputes about the covenant throughout the history of the church (e.g. in the time of Cocceius, in the nineteenth century, during the second world war in the Netherlands). They dismiss these disputes as theological hairsplitting and a waste of time. Now, I would be the last one to deny that much of the squabbling was fruitless. All the same, I must point out that the issue at stake was the unity of the covenant, a doctrine essential to the health and welfare of the church.

Those who have only a vague understanding of the covenant will not be in a position to resist the errors of the dispensationalists. If they reject the view that the covenant remains substantially the same (even in the life to come), they will be powerless when confronted with Darby's modern successors—in part because today's dispensationalists conceal their great debt to Darby.

The church in brackets?

If the dispensational grace covers only the New Testament era and some centuries beyond it, we cannot speak of the church in the time of the old covenant. There was no church in those days. Pentecost is then declared the church's birthday. And the church comes to an end with the Rapture—when the Christians suddenly disappear from the earth. There will still be some history after that—in fact, very lively history—but there will no longer be a church on earth. Hence the dispensationalists sometimes speak of the present as the "church age."

Their outlook can be depicted schematically as follows:

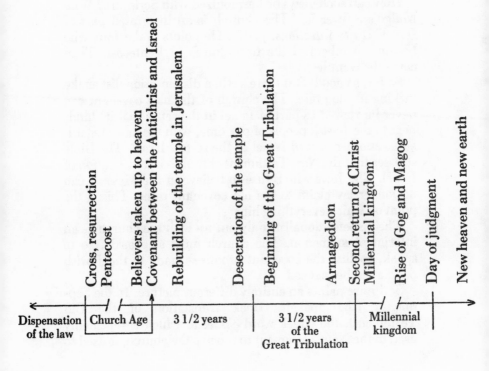

Why is it emphasized so heavily that we live in the "church age" and that this age will come to an end before long? Because the dispensationalists believe that the church actually represents an interruption, something that stands between the Old Testament prophecies and their fulfillment. In redemptive history, the "church age" must be put between brackets. The church is something temporary, an interim phenomenon coming between the historical kingdom of David and the future Davidic kingdom. In the latter kingdom, the promises made to Israel will be fulfilled literally—in an era in which the church has disappeared from the earth.

According to this standpoint, the church is put between brackets; it is merely transitory. Moreover, the church is not the mother of all believers. We await another mother—a Jewish mother!

How can such views be harmonized with Scripture? Wim Malgo's answer is: "The Church is an integrated part of Israel" (*Fifty Questions,* p. 12). He points to the Jews who became members of the first church at Pentecost. Then came the Gentiles.

So far, so good. But there's still a dispensationalist snake lurking in the grass. The church of the new covenant can never be viewed as part of Israel in the sense that it stands next to the Jewish people of our time, with the latter regarded as another part of Israel or the rest of Israel. The Bible stresses that the New Testament church is a *continuation* of Israel. The Jews who refuse to believe in the Messiah can no longer lay claim to the old covenant titles. This is the point on which everything hinges.

The dispensationalists only put up with the church as an interim phenomenon. The church must step aside, so to speak, so that the covenant promises made to the Jewish people can be realized.

Scripture paints an entirely different picture. In the Septuagint (the ancient Greek translation of the Old Testament), the Greek word *ekklésia,* which is repeatedly used in the New Testament to refer to the church, is used to translate the Hebrew word *qahal*, which refers to the congregation or assembly of Israel. The church is a continuation of Israel as an assembled people united through its ties to the Lord. To say that the church is somehow "new" that it "begins" at Pentecost, is to fly in the face of God's clear revelation. The church has been present on earth since the very beginning of the world and will continue to exist until we see Jesus return. Jesus did not *found* the church while He was on earth—although He did allow His chosen people on earth to constitute themselves as a new kind of body.

The dispensationalist distinction between Israel and the "church" (which is then graciously allowed to become part of Israel) also conflicts with another Scriptural given: the New Testament church is sometimes called a "people."

In Exodus 19:5, which gives us the theme of the entire Penteteuch, we read that Israel is to be God's "own possession among all peoples." Paul uses this text in Titus 2:14, where he writes that Christ "gave himself for us to redeem us from all iniquity and to purify for himself a people of his own." Exodus 19:5-6 also shines through in I Peter 2:9: "But you are a chosen race, a royal priesthood, a holy nation, God's own people." In the following text Peter goes on to declare: "Once you were no people, but now you are God's people" (see also Hos. 1:10).

To get a proper grasp of the implications, we must go back to the Greek text. The word Peter chose when he spoke of "God's people" was not *ethnos* (i.e. a people as an ethnic unit, a nation) but *laos*. In the Septuagint, *laos* is used to translate the Hebrew word *am*, which is the term used to refer to Israel as the covenant people.

Laos is a very old Greek word. Although it was used by Homer, it eventually slipped into virtual oblivion. In Jewish circles it remained alive, of course, because of its use in the Septuagint.

The Jews got into the habit of referring to themselves as the "laos" of the Hebrews. As a result, the Gentiles picked up this term again and started using it as a name for the

Jews. In Miletus there was a theater in which the fifth row
of seats was officially set aside for the "laos" of the Jews
and their "God-fearing" Gentile co-religionists. Even the
Jews began to use the word *laos* in this more restricted
sense, e.g. on stone coffins. The synagogue at Sardis had a
blessing for the "laos." (It was not regarded as necessary to
state explicitly that the Jews were meant.)

What about the New Testament? It applies this term,
which was already in use in the synagogue, to the church.
"I have many people (*laos*) in this city," Christ says to Paul
(Acts 18:10). In Revelation 18:4 we read: "Come out of her,
my people (*laos*)." If Israel persists in its refusal to believe
in Jesus as the Messiah, it will no longer be God's "laos."
"Every soul that does not listen to that prophet [Christ]
shall be destroyed from the people (*laos*)," declares Peter
(Acts 3:23; see also Lev. 23:29; Deut. 18:15, 18-19). The
church is "God's own *laos*."

We do violence to Scripture when we speak of a separate
"church age" and regard today's Jews as part of God's
covenant people. The Old Testament period was a "church
age" too. And the time after Christ's return will be a
"church age." Sabbath rest awaits the *laos* of God. That
laos is the church of all ages.

The fact of the matter is that Darbyist dispensationalism
contains a hidden element of hostility toward the church.
This hostility is rooted in its sympathy for Judaism.

"If I forget you, O Jerusalem . . ." (Ps. 137:5). "Peace be
in Israel!" (Ps. 125:5). We should apply such texts to the
church, but the dispensationalists read them as pointing to
the restoration of Israel and the golden future of a
Palestinian Jerusalem.

What we really face here is a Zionizing of Christian hope.
If we yield to it, our sense of the church's place will be
weakened. What else would you expect from such an
outlook?

Isn't that what Darby had in mind all along? To him the
church was Babylon. Here again we see that dispensationalism is a revolutionary doctrine at heart.

What about the "today of grace"?

The Heidelberg Catechism is correct in teaching that the church is being gathered from the beginning of the world to the very end (Lord's Day 21). According to the Arminians, there might well come a time when there are no believers on earth, despite Christ's death on the cross. The Canons of Dordt, which have much more to say to our time than people sometimes realize, declare that this false teaching "contradicts the article of faith according to which we believe the catholic Christian Church" (Chapter 2, Rejection of Errors, Paragraph 1).

In Darbyism and dispensationalism, this Arminian doctrine rears its head again: when the Rapture comes, all the believers will be taken up to heaven. Thus there will be no believers left on earth. The *possibility* left open by the Arminians becomes a *certainty*.

The dispensationalists also teach that there are various dispensations in which man is given an opportunity to demonstrate his willingness to obey God. Man's reaction leads God to introduce dispensation after dispensation.

Some dispensationalists even distinguish between three churches: the church of Matthew 16:18, the Peter church of Acts, and the mystery church of the letters Paul wrote as a captive. Today's church is the mystery church. But this latest "attempt" on God's part will also come to an end; the mystery church will not be around anymore when the events on earth reach their culmination. God has a different plan in mind for the seven-year kingdom, and yet another plan for the millennial kingdom to follow it.

The doctrine that today's church is an interim phenomenon, a church in brackets, has extensive implications for Christian conduct and attitudes. All the emphasis falls on the "kingdoms" to come, in which the Old Testament prophecies will be fulfilled.

When dispensationalism pushes the church aside, the centrality and significance of preaching is also undermined. The time in which we live is no longer seen as decisive, for there will be other periods, periods in which conversion is still possible. Because hopes are fixed on future "dispensations," the powerful appeal made in New Testament preaching is weakened. The New Testament declares plainly: "I tell you, *now* is the time of God's favor, *now* is the day of salvation" (II Cor. 6:2 NIV; see also Is. 49:6). "Exhort one another *every day*, as long as it is called 'today' " (Heb. 3:13).

Dispensationalism obscures the definitive, absolute character of the day of salvation, the "today of grace." As the moment of decision is moved ahead to other dispensations, we are reminded of the doctrine of purgatory. Man still has a chance to set things right in some vague future age. At bottom dispensationalism is an *escapism* with little love for the church.

Two kingdoms?

The dispensationalists distinguish between the kingdom of heaven and the kingdom of God. In the Gospel according to Matthew, the term *kingdom of heaven* is used regularly, but Luke uses *kingdom of God*. Now, these terms really refer to one and the same kingdom, as we see from Matthew 19:23-4, where both are found.

The dispensationalists make the kingdom of heaven into a Jewish kingdom that will arise after Christ's first return. The "kingdom of God" is the eventual complete fulfillment that comes later. The "church age" is a dispensation of the kingdom of God—but it has nothing to do with the kingdom of heaven. The kingdom of God is a *spiritual*, universal kingdom.

What we face here is more than an irresponsible reading of the text in which separate, distinct meanings are attached to equivalent terms: we also see a Gnostic version of mysticism coming to the fore. The Gnostics teach that the world was created by some other god. What really matters to them is "spirit." And mystics, of course, also despise creation and engage in spiritualization.

Dispensationalism wants to read Scripture literally. Therefore the unfulfilled prophecies must be fulfilled in the kingdom of heaven and take on an *earthly* form. The kingdom of God, on the other hand, is spiritual in form, and so is the "church age." This spiritual form is the reason why the realization of the (earthly) kingdom of heaven must be postponed until after the interim age of the church.

Thus the dispensationalists are busy cutting, separating, tearing apart. The covenant is ripped to pieces. The church becomes one of God's temporary ways of dealing with man. And the kingdom of God becomes a spiritual entity that apparently has nothing to do with the Davidic kingdom.

We read in Luke 1:32-3 that Jesus will be given the throne of His father David and that He will be King over the house of David forever. The dispensationalists apply this text to Jesus' rule in the millennial kingdom, i.e. the "kingdom of heaven." But how is this interpretation to be harmonized with the assurance that there will be no end to His kingdom? (Luke 1:33). That we are not told.

Perhaps we can ignore such a text, but it doesn't go away. There it stands, pointing out the error of the scholastic distinction between nature and grace as drawn by the dispensationalists.

Paul also tells us about the kingship of Jesus Christ: "He must reign until he has put all his enemies under his feet" (I Cor. 15:25). When Paul talks about Jesus as King, he isn't referring to a kingship over the church *plus* a kingship over the house of Jacob. Jesus is King of the church—and the church is the house of Jacob. At the same time, He is King over the entire creation. Thus His kingship is not to be understood in spiritualistic terms.

Reading the Bible and singing psalms would become difficult if we were governed by the distorted dispensationalist understanding of covenant, church and kingdom: we would then have to think of the contemporary state of Israel and of the Jews as a race whenever we read or sang about the people of Israel, the house of Jacob, or the descendants of

Abraham. These names that occur so often in the psalms and hymns we sing point to a period beyond the "church age," according to the Darbyists and dispensationalists. Apparently Christ is not yet king over the house of Jacob!

The dispensationalists on the seven-year period

In article 19 of Dallas Theological Seminary's "Doctrinal Statement" we read:

> We believe that the translation of the church will be followed by the fulfillment of Israel's seventieth week (Dan. 9:27; Rev. 6:1—9:21) during which the church, the body of Christ, will be in heaven. The whole period of Israel's seventieth week will be a time of judgment on the whole earth, at the end of which the times of the Gentiles will be brought to a close. The latter half of this period will be the time of Jacob's trouble (Jer. 30:7), which our Lord called the great tribulation (Matt. 24:15-21). We believe that the universal righteousness will not be realized previous to the second coming of Christ, but that the world is day by day ripening for the judgment and that the age will end with a fearful apostasy.

This article gives us a summary of dispensationalist doctrine. The following points are mentioned:

a) The time after the "church age" is the seventieth week of Daniel 9:27. By then the church has disappeared from the earth.
b) Revelation 6-19 deals with that time. Thus nothing is said about the church in those chapters of Scripture.
c) The Great Tribulation begins 3 1/2 years after the end of the "church age."
d) The world is getting worse and worse. It will end after a period of fearful apostasy.

In the next four sections, I will take up these points one by one.

Daniel's seventieth week

In Daniel 9 we read that Daniel was studying the book of Jeremiah, which contained a promise that Jerusalem would be restored after 70 years. Because this promise had not yet been fulfilled, Daniel prayed to the Lord about Jerusalem's plight.

After this prayer Daniel was told by the angel Gabriel that the 70 years are "seventy weeks of years." Thus it would be much longer than Daniel expected before the glorious restoration came about. The return to Jerusalem and the initial restoration of the services in the temple would take seven "weeks." After that the reconstruction of Jerusalem would continue, but it would be a "troubled time." After the sixty-second week, an anointed one would be "cut off." This is a reference to the temporary interruption in the legitimate priestly services during the days of Antiochus Epiphanes.

Daniel 9 also speaks of a strange people destroying the city and the sanctuary, with their tyranny lasting one "week." Halfway through that "week," the sacrifices and offerings would be halted.

The *Scofield Reference Bible* comments on this passage as follows:

> The "he" of verse 27 is the "prince that shall come" of verse 26, whose people (Rome) destroyed the temple, A.D. 70. He is the same with the "little horn" of chapter 7. He will covenant with the Jews to restore their temple sacrifices for one week (seven years), but in the middle of that time he will break the covenant and fulfill Dan. 12:11; II Thess. 2:3, 4.

According to this view, Daniel 9:26 is talking about the destruction of Jerusalem by the *Romans*—and not the events in the time of Antiochus Epiphanes. And verse 27 is to be read as applying to the *future*. The "prince who is to come" (vs. 26) is the "he" of verse 27, the Roman dictator who will allow the temple services in Jerusalem to be restored again at some point in the future. But after 3 1/2 years he will show his true colors and allow the desolating sacrilege to be established (see Matt. 24:15). He will even go so far as to set himself up as a god (see II Thess. 2:4).

To make some room for the fulfillment of this prophecy, the dispensationalists maintain that there will be an *interim period* after the sixty-ninth week—the "church age." The *Scofield Reference Bible* tells us: "Between the sixty-ninth week, after which Messiah was cut off, and the seventieth week, within which the 'little horn' of Dan. 7 will run his awful course, intervenes this entire "Church Age." Thus there must be a gap between "weeks" 69 and 70. By now that gap has lasted almost 2000 years.

When we read Daniel 9:26-7 without preconceptions, we see that verse 27 is a further explication of verse 26. For this reason alone, the view that verse 27 refers to distant future events must be rejected. The two verses are talking about the same period of time—the age of Antiochus Epiphanes. There is no justification for smuggling in a "church age" because of a supposed chronological difference between verses 26 and 27.

There is another point to be made in this context. The expectation of a future rebuilding of the temple is also to be found in various church fathers. Those church fathers read Daniel 9:27 as well as Matthew 24 and II Thessalonians 2 as prophecies still awaiting fulfillment. In other words, they read these passages as applying to what lies ahead. But they never went so far as to invent a "church age," nor did they talk about a seven-year period or a millennial kingdom in which the Jews would occupy center stage. The so-called Letter of Barnabas, which is often accused of Chiliasm, contains some harsh words directed *against* the Jews.

The book of Revelation and the period after the "church age"

The dispensationalists maintain that Revelation 4:1 (or 6:1) through 19:21 deals with a period that begins after the believers are taken up to heaven. This view is no better founded than the view that there is a "church-age" between "weeks" 69 and 70.

The dispensationalists apply the messages to the *seven* churches to the "church age." (Think of the *seven* ages of the church!) The visions that follow the seven messages are then applied to the time after the "church age." This procedure breaks up the book of Revelation into two parts: (1) the messages, which are meant for the "church age," and (2) the visions, which apply to the time after the "church age."

There is no justification for breaking up the book of Revelation in such a way. The Apocalypse of John is a single, unified book. Of course one can distinguish between chapters 1-3 and chapters 4-22—as long as the book is not broken into two separate books. The second part of the book of Revelation casts light on the first. The entire book is concerned with the church on earth—starting with the seven congregations for whom the seven messages were meant.

In Revelation 1:19 we read: "Now write what you see, what is and what is to take place hereafter." This text has led some scholars to divide the book of Revelation as follows:

a) "what you see" — the visions of chapter 1
b) "what is" — the seven messages
c) "what is to take place hereafter—the visions of chapters 4-22

This division has set its stamp on the interpretation of the book of Revelation and has done much to advance the view that the book deals with events that are still to come.

There is plenty of reason to reject this division. A careful look at the seven messages shows that they contain a covenantal message not just for the time in which they were written but also for the *future*. And in the visions we read references to events in the *past* (12:15; 5:6).

In a brilliant article entitled "A Formula Describing Prophecy," W. C. van Unnik has shown that Revelation 1:19 is simply an instance of a well-established mode of expression (*Novum Testamentum*, IX, 1962-63, pp. 86-94). Such a formula involving the past, the present and the future is characteristic of prophecy. In The Wisdom of Solomon, an apocryphal book, Solomon declares that God made known to him "the beginning and end and middle of times" (7:18). He uses words that we also find in the book of Revelation—*arché* (beginning) and *telos* (end). The same trinity of past, present and future appears in one of God's titles: God is the One "who is and who was and who is to come" (Rev. 1:4,8).

The words of Revelation 1:19 were never intended to serve as a clue for dividing the book into three parts. What they indicate instead is that the entire book of Revelation is to be read as *prophecy*—a message already spelled out in verse 3. Thus the seven messages are prophecy as well as the visions.

The presence of these visions at the end of the Bible does not give us any right to take giant apocalyptic leaps and build dispensationalist sand castles in the air. We may not cut the book of Revelation into two parts and apply everything from chapter 6 on to the future or the "end time," even though many believers and interpreters have long done exactly that. Such an approach is arbitrary.

The Apocalypse of John comes to us as *one* book. Therefore the visions belong with the early chapters. This comes out clearly in the similarities between the visions and the early chapters. (Think of the references to the throne of satan, false prophecy, and white garments.) The visions are a further illustration of the message addressed by the King to the seven churches; they are a figurative portrayal of that message on an enlarged scale.

People who lived 2000 years ago were accustomed to seeing "ordinary" things depicted in grandiose terms. The altar at Pergamum was built when the dynasty of Pergamum conquered the Galatians. Did this altar to Zeus have a Napoleonic-style battlefield portrayed on it? No, it pictured the gods of Mount Olympus instead, as they did battle with giants. The victory over the Galatians was depicted in visionary—indeed, "apocalyptic"—terms, i.e. in the form of a *gigantomachy.*

Isn't that just what the book of Revelation also does? When God gives us His revelation, He makes use of elements drawn from our own experience to get the message across. The struggle of the young churches in Asia Minor against the synagogue of satan is depicted in visions, with a "gigantomachy" as background (see Rev. 12, 13, 19).

The widespread interpretation of Revelation 4-22 as a treatment of *future* events ("what is to take place hereafter") has created a climate in which strange apocalyptic ideas (many of them bearing a strong resemblance to worldly apocalyptic thinking) flourish. We could speak here of a secularizing or politicizing of Scripture.

That's all the more reason why the last book of the Bible is worthy of renewed attention in our time. Revelation is a covenantal book and must be interpreted as such. It is not a timetable spelling out the future.

The Great Tribulation

When I contemplate the picture of the future drawn by the dispensationalists, I can't help but be reminded of a pop-art collage. Materials are brought together from diverse sources and pasted down side by side to create a stunning effect.

Now, there are some people who are greatly impressed by such an outlook on the future. They hunger for predictions, for some sort of authoritative voice to tell them what lies ahead. The pop-apocalypse of the dispensationalists gives them what they are looking for. In our consumer society, dispensationalist literature about the future strikes a responsive chord in the hearts of thousands.

Dallas Theological Seminary's "Doctrinal Statement"

speaks of "the time of Jacob's troubles," using this phrase out of context (see Jer. 30:7). This text is then pasted down right next to Matthew 24:15-21. Both passages are read as statements about the seven-year period and the Great Tribulation scheduled to begin halfway through that period. We are told that Christ's authority stands behind this vision of the future: "The latter part of this period [i.e. the seven years after the Rapture] will be the time of Jacob's trouble, which *our Lord* called the great tribulation."

There is an artist at work behind the scenes here: everything is presented in an objective, seemingly realistic style that a photographer might strive for. This vision of the future with all its predictions has tremendous appeal. Otherwise Dallas could not send this colorful collage into the world as its doctrinal statement.

What we face here is a piece of dispensationalist propaganda. The texts quoted in support of this eschatology are used in a misleading way.

Let's look first at Jeremiah 30:7. Does it apply to some troubled time yet to come? From the context it is clear that Jeremiah is talking about *Judah* passing through a time of trouble or distress before it emerges from exile. G. C. Aalders comments on this passage as follows: "When the prophet Jeremiah, in his own colorful way, sketches the great tribulation at hand, he must mean the tribulation of Jerusalem's imminent destruction." What if someone were to argue that Jeremiah must mean a future day of judgment since he says, "That day is so great there is none like it"? Aalders rejects this argument: "It can be said of any day of special misfortune that it is a great day, a day without parallel" (see his commentary on Jeremiah in the "Korte Verklaring" series).

We must resist the temptation to lift an intriguing text out of its context and make it part of our apocalyptic collage. This applies to Matthew 24:15-21 just as much as Jeremiah 30:7.

The passage in Matthew deals with the anxious days

before the second destruction of Jerusalem in A.D. 70. This is clear from the terms Jesus uses—"those who are *in Judea*" (vs. 16); "Pray that your flight may not be in winter or *on a sabbath*" (vs. 20). The text itself rules out the prospect of applying this passage to the distant future. And the text must be our guide, after all. Thus we need not sit back and wait for Matthew 24:15-21 to be fulfilled.

Unfortunately, there are many exegetes and preachers who do apply this passage from Matthew 24 directly to eschatological events leading up to the day of judgment. In some Bibles Matthew 24 is given a misleading heading, e.g. "Discourse about the last things." With such headings right in the Bibles people read every day, is it any wonder that it is widely assumed that Jesus is talking about the end of time in Matthew 24? The dispensationalist dogma of the coming Great Tribulation builds on this foundation. (I will come back to this point in Chapter 5.)

Reasons for pessimism?

"The age will end with a fearful apostasy," we are told by Dallas Theological Seminary. Isn't that true? Don't we see it with our own eyes? Doesn't I Timothy 4:1 tell us that there are difficult days awaiting us in the "later times"? "Now the Spirit expressly says that in later times some will depart from the faith by giving heed to deceitful spirits and doctrines of demons." In Jude's letter we read about evil men defiling the flesh and rejecting authority (vs. 8).

The words of Scripture are not to be denied or ignored, of course. But what are those "later days"? What is the last hour?

From Peter's Pentecost sermon, it is apparent that the "later days" *began* with the outpouring of the Holy Spirit (Acts 2:17). For us "the end of the ages has come" (I Cor. 10:11). John writes: "Children, it is the last hour" (I John 2:18).

Now, it has been fashionable for years to divide the New

Testament era into "latter days" and the "very last days" or
the "end time." When prophecies from Daniel and Matthew 24 were applied to the latter days—and not just in sectarian circles—the result was the conviction that things are
getting worse and worse. Whenever horrible things happen,
people nod their heads knowingly and say to each other:
"It's all foretold in the Bible. These are signs that the end is
near."

But the New Testament teaches that Christ will return
like a thief in the night, when people are telling each other
that everything is in order (I Thess. 5). If there is to be a
special "end time" heralded by all sorts of clear signs, we'll
have to correct I Thessalonians 5:2-3.

I must add that when I reject the widespread pessimism
about the time before Christ's return, I am not choosing for
a postmillennial position. In other words, I do not believe
in inevitable progress toward a much better world in this
dispensation (see Loraine Boettner, *The Millennium*,
Philadelphia, 1957, p. 136). But the postmillennialists are
right in rejecting the idea of a special "end time" or "latter
days" as a period of great horror.

The belief in a perceptible evolution and growth of evil is
based not on Biblical prophecy but on extra-Biblical sources—newspaper reports, statistical analyses of crime, our
subjective experiences, and so forth. In some people this
belief calls forth an active response: they want to do battle
with evil. Others take a more passive attitude: in a fatalistic
frame of mind, they await the *Götterdämmerung*, the
destruction of our global civilization. On the basis of Bible
texts torn from their context and reports presented by the
news media, people predict that the end cannot be far away
and point to greater horrors yet to come.

That these pessimists have the best of intentions and
even believe that Scripture is on their side I do not deny for
a moment. All the same, we must recognize this attitude for
what it is, namely, a revolutionary escapism that flees the
here-and-now, sees no more promises to cling to, and waits
for the overthrow of all that is good and just.

Our God is not a God of revolution. Because He is the God of creation, He loves the continuity and meaningful development of the historical process. He works out His purposes by making use of families and successive generations. He is the God of Noah, the God who gives us the rainbow to assure us that He will never again destroy the world with a flood. He is the God of Abraham, Isaac and Jacob, the God of the covenant. In times of need and peril, He stands by His people, blessing them and giving them reason to rejoice. That applies to our time too.

"Humble yourselves under the mighty hand of God," Peter tells us. Why? So that "in due time he may *exalt* you" (I Pet. 5:6).

Our God is also the God of Elijah. He preserves a church for Himself and guards His own in the storms that rage around them.

His church has no right to take an optimistic, triumphalistic attitude. It was not without reason that Luther ended his 95 Theses with a reminder that we enter the kingdom only through many tribulations.

We must not stand on the sidelines with scowls on our faces, ready to give up as soon as the panic begins. Such an unnatural and ahistorical attitude would succeed only in robbing us of our strength. Instead we must work as long as it is day.

Let's not be frightened by people who point to the signs of the times and tell us that things are getting worse and worse. Yahweh remembers His covenant. That covenant is sure, for our God stands by the promises He has made.

Interpreting Biblical Prophecy

Hal Lindsey

Against the background of our understanding of dispensationalism, we will now take a closer look at Hal Lindsey's book *The Late Great Planet Earth* (PE), published in 1970. I will also draw on the material in *There's a New World Coming* (NW).

Who is Hal Lindsey? He was born in Houston, Texas in 1930. During the Korean War he served in the U.S. Coast Guard. After the war he became a tugboat captain on the Mississippi. He admits that he used to live it up those days, but he was converted through Bible reading. He had already been baptized three times (at 11, 14, and 16) in three different churches, but baptism seemed to have little influence on his life.

His reading of the Bible and a near accident on the Mississippi did make a difference, however. One day he heard a 2 1/2 hour sermon on the conflict in the Middle East and became convinced that the Bible is indeed the inspired Word of God. As a result he began reading the Bible six to eight hours per day (in addition to his work). He believed because of the political "fulfillments" of the prophecies. It turned out that the Bible was right after all!

Lindsey decided to study at Dalles Theological Seminary. Perhaps it was someone connected with the Seminary who had delivered that long sermon on the conflict in the Middle East. He was immediately admitted to the Seminary in Dallas, and his financial needs were miraculously taken care of.

46

In 1961 he received the Master of Theology degree. Then he went to work for Campus Crusade. Currently he is in charge of the Light and Powerhouse in Los Angeles, which is a training center for pastoral workers.

The Late Great Planet Earth made him famous. It has been translated into at least 20 languages (including Swahili). He has also written a number of other books.

In *The Incredible Cover-Up* (Plainfield, N.Y., 1975), Dave MacPherson records an important comment that he found in *The Jesus People: Old-Time Religion in the Age of Aquarius*. When the "Jesus people" arose as a significant offshoot of the counterculture of the 1960s, it became apparent that many Christian young people no longer believed that the believers will be taken up to heaven *before* the Great Tribulation. These "hippie" Christians had no money to buy dispensationalist books. All they had to read was the Bible. As a result, they wound up believing that the believers will be taken up to heaven *after* the Great Tribulation. In American theology, this standpoint is known as post-tribulationism (the "post-trib" position).

The effects of this development were felt in Dallas. The newly converted students on campus had not been indoctrinated in the "pre-trib" position. The situation was getting out of hand. It looked as though the rising generation would not adhere to the "pre-trib" position that typified Dallas Theological Seminary. That would mean a sharp decline in Dallas's tremendous influence on education and evangelism.

What could be done about this? Was there anyone who was familiar with the "Jesus people" as well as the "pre-trib" position and could write in such a way that young people would again accept the "pre-trib" standpoint and fight for it? Yes, there was someone both willing and able. Moreover, this young man, whose name was Hal Lindsey, was even a graduate of the Seminary in Dallas! (see MacPherson's book, pp. 131-2).

Thus Lindsey, who had learned his theology at Dallas,

became an apologist for the Dallas school of thought. He has been hailed as a long-haired reincarnation of Scofield. Events have proven that he was just the man to reassert Dallas's influence over the new generation.

Now, Hal Lindsey will not be remembered as one of the outstanding theologians of our time. He was not an outstanding student in the Seminary either. It's not likely that his classmates expected him to write a best seller someday. Yet, given his simple way of speaking and some professional help from a journalist, he managed to strike just the right note. Because he made it sound so convincing, he satisfied the great hunger for "religious" leadership—especially on the part of people who have little or nothing to do with the church. Lindsey quickly became the top popularizer of the dispensationalist approach to Biblical prophecy.

In Daniel 12:9 we read: "The words are shut up and sealed until the time of the end." Lindsey interprets this text to mean that many Biblical prophecies would remain a mystery until the time of the end actually arrived. In our own time, he argues, the meaning of the Biblical prophecies is finally being unlocked and explained in all sorts of publications.

Lindsey admits that he draws on the work of Bible scholars of the last three centuries who devoted themselves to the study of Biblical prophecy. These earlier scholars could see the time of fulfillment coming. Today's generation is the "terminal generation"—a phrase Lindsey uses as the title of one of his books. Such comments on Lindsey's part have made a tremendous impression on the public.

Lindsey has also visited Europe and made a hit there. There were already dispensationalist groups in Europe; their work and influence paved the way for him. Yet, dispensationalism was a mere undercurrent in Europe. Lindsey managed to bring it to the surface suddenly and win tremendous popularity and attention for it.

Lindsey wants nothing to do with Biblical criticism, and

he is also opposed to the charismatic movement and the theology of the World Council of Churches. By taking these positions, he gains the trust of many "evangelicals" and wins a warm reception for his outlook on Biblical prophecy.

Because Lindsey has made such a stir in orthodox, evangelical circles, his writings deserve a closer look. Does he read his own message into the Bible when he throws all those Scripture references at his readers? Or is he truly letting the Word speak?

Some of the points taken up earlier will be touched on again as we examine Lindsey's views. Moreover, we will see that the widely accepted interpretation of the book of Revelation lends a lot of support to the dispensationalist way of thinking. In the concluding chapters of this book, therefore, I will raise the question whether our reading of John's Apocalypse is in need of revision and correction.

A relative difference?

On the back cover of *There's a New World Coming,* we find a photograph of Hal Lindsey and his wife, with England's famous Stonehenge in the background. Beneath the picture we read:

> Through these stones, 4000 years ago, priests could site the sun, moon and stars and predict with exact accuracy the seasons, sun risings and eclipses of the sun and moon . . . . There have been many, throughout the centuries of man's long history, who have sought to predict the course of human events, but none have had the incredible accuracy of the ancient Hebrew prophets.

Before we even open the book, then, we have reason to be suspicious. The Old Testament prophets are being put on the same level as heathen priests, although Lindsey's preference is clearly for the prophets of the Bible. Like it or not, the comparative religion approach is already introduced on the cover of the book.

Now, someone might respond by arguing that what appears on the cover of a book is generally the publisher's responsibility—not the author's. That may be, but when we open *The Late Great Planet Earth*, we also read interesting comments about astrology, spiritualism, clairvoyancy, and other such phenomena. Lindsey finally concludes:

> However, compared to the speculation of most that is called prophetic today, the Bible contains clear and unmistakable prophetic signs. We are able to see right now in this Best Seller predictions made centuries ago being fulfilled before our eyes.
> The Bible makes fantastic claims; but these claims are no more startling than those of present day astrologers, prophets and seers. Furthermore, the claims of the Bible have a greater basis in historical evidence and fact (PE, 7).

It appears, then, that Scriptural prophecy differs from the prophecy of the "seers" mainly in that it is more accurate. There is more historical evidence to back it up. The relationship of heathendom to Christianity is a relationship of less to more.

Here a fundamental error is being made, for Scripture is unique and cannot be compared to the horoscopes and fanciful stories concocted by soothsayers. Scripture is not simply the highest peak in a mountain range of prophecy. The prophecy we find in Scripture is unique; it does not fit into the same class as any extra-Biblical prophecy. What did Elijah have in common with the prophets of Baal? Was he just like them, but a little better at his trade?

Hal Lindsey's starting point, then, is completely wrong. But there is more to be said.

Prophesying and foretelling the future

Because Lindsey, following his comparative religion approach, puts Biblical prophecy on the same level as the prophecies of people like Edgar Cayce and Jeanne Dixon, he loses sight of the element that makes Biblical prophecy *unique*. According to him, Biblical prophecy is just a matter of predicting the future. In this regard he stands by Darby's thesis that prophecy is prewritten history.

One can easily see that the prophets were right on target when they predicted Israel's exile, the destruction of Babylon (two political events), and the birth of Christ. Lindsey devotes entire pages to describing how Biblical prophecies have come true. He writes: "Bible prophecy can become a sure foundation upon which your faith can grow—and there is no need to shelve your intellect while finding this faith" (PE, 7). Thus, an intellectual approach to Biblical prophecy leads to the conclusion that it must be accepted. Why? Because it is actually being fulfilled.

Now, is it really true that the Biblical prophets were making predictions, that they were foretelling the future? Not at all.

The prophet speaks the Word of God. He appeals to his people to be true to Yahweh, the God of the covenant. Thus he functions within a covenant context. He comes to his people with a threat or with words of comfort. Insofar as his message touches on the future, he does point to events down the road. But the prophet never makes predictions as such. His message is conditional; it is tied in with God's promises, on the one hand, and His threats, on the other.

It is striking that Hal Lindsey has virtually nothing to say about the covenant. When he talks about Israel (God's covenant people), he uses the vague term *the Jewish people* (see PE, 19). This term is a link in the chain of his argument; he uses it later to tie in the Old Testament prophecies with the modern state of Israel (see PE, 32-47).

I will return to this point later. At present I am concerned with Lindsey's fundamental error—he does not take the covenant into account and therefore looks at Biblical prophecy as a single example of a broader species called "prophecy," i.e. human predictions about the future.

The point we must not lose sight of is that Biblical

prophecy is something unique. The Bible leaves room for seers and soothsayers operating outside Israel's covenant community—but it does not recognize them as *prophets*. True prophecy was possible only within the covenant context. Of course there were also false prophets at work within the covenant community. In fact, false prophecy in the strict sense was *only* possible within the covenant context.

The false prophets presented flattering visions of a glorious future, while failing to acknowledge that Israel's future depended on its response to God's covenant demands. They cried, "Peace! Peace!" and did not concern themselves with Israel's apostasy. They painted a bright picture of the future, but they did not spell out the conditions Israel would have to accept if those visions were ever to become reality. Through their lies, they promoted a false sense of security.

The true prophets constantly held the demands of the covenant before Israel. They threatened Israel with God's covenant wrath and tried to lure their people to obedience by dangling the covenant promises before them. When they talked about the future, it was never to present detached predictions about what would take place. Their talk of the future always fell within the framework of a covenantal appeal for reformation.

The true prophets were not concerned with authenticating their prophecies by presenting predictions that came true. In fact, some of their predictions didn't come true at all. When Micah prophesied that Jerusalem would be plowed as a field and turn into a heap of ruins, his words led to repentance under King Hezekiah. As a result, the Lord held back the judgment He had in mind (Mic. 3:12; Jer. 26:17-19). The same thing happened when Jonah preached in Nineveh. Once Nineveh repented, the Lord changed His mind about the judgment He had planned.

When Hal Lindsey looks at a Biblical prophecy, he misses its covenant context and fails to realize that the words of the prophet were meant as an appeal to God's people to change their ways. He makes foretelling the future basic to prophecy and therefore loses sight of the central thrust.

We are left with the impression that Biblical prophecy is intended to satisfy our curiosity about the future. Now, if this were indeed the purpose, one would have to judge Biblical prophecy in the same terms as the efforts of heathen priests and soothsayers who have sought to tell us what the future has in store. And that's just what Lindsey does. In effect, he drags the Lord's prophets down to the level of the heathen seers—even though he hopes to prove that Biblical prophecy is of greater value because so many of the predictions made by the Bible's prophets have already come true.

Homemade prophecy for sale

Hal Lindsey uncovers prophetic puzzles everywhere in the Bible. Locked within these puzzles are specific predictions about the future. He proceeds from the assumption that the prophets have written an almanac for us so that we will know what lies ahead. If we apply our minds to the puzzles and solve them logically, we will learn just what the future has in store for us. "We are able to see right now in this Best Seller predictions made centuries ago being fulfilled before our eyes" (PE, 7).

In his books, Hal Lindsey uses Biblical prophecy to open a supermarket in which he sells the curious inside information about the near future, especially World War III. He gets his material from Daniel and Revelation, Ezekiel and Matthew 24. Come, buy and read! There's no need to be uncertain about the future any longer! We can see "right now" that the Bible's prophecies are "being fulfilled before our eyes."

Apparently the prophets who lived in Bible times had their binoculars focused on our time, on the 1970s and 1980s. We are truly privileged to be living in such times! Earlier ages lived in darkness. Now, through deductions from what the Biblical prophets tell us, great light has been shed on the future. We jump from one best seller prediction to another. Lindsey argues: ". . . a person can be given a secure and yet exciting view of his destiny by making an honest investigation of the tested truth of Bible prophecy" (PE, 8).

Put the emphasis on the word *exciting*. And remember that these truths are "tested"; they come with a guarantee! We could not possibly be deceived. Just as prophecies came true in the old days, they will come true in our time. Thus Lindsey uses a demagogue's argument to sell his views.

We might well ask: have the prophecies of Hal Lindsey been tested? Have his predictions come true? No! We're still waiting for the fulfillment. Moreover, as I pointed out above, Lindsey proceeds from mistaken notions about the role and function of the Old Testament prophets.

Unfortunately, an uncritical public seems blind to these flaws in Lindsey's approach. Eagerly they devour his views. Lindsey slays his millions with his clever approach. "Tested truths of Biblical prophecy!" He gives the Bible his personal backing: the Bible is right after all! Lindsey seeks to lead his readers to the same conversion experience he underwent himself.

A danger to Christianity

It is my conviction that Hal Lindsey's work will harm the cause of the gospel. First of all, his prophecies cannot be defended on Biblical grounds, as I will show later in the book. His entire view of "prophecy" is at odds with the Bible's view. And don't think this will escape the attention of outsiders. They see Christians performing acrobatic stunts as they twist Bible texts to fit some modern prophet's vision of the future. How can outsiders help but get a poor impression of Christianity that way? Furthermore, when Lindsey's prophecies fail to come true—and some of them have been awaiting fulfillment for a long time already—the resulting disillusionment will hardly serve to glorify God.

When Christians turn the Bible into a book of puzzles (puzzles for which there are instant answers if we can only find the clue), they turn the gospel into a secret teaching to be understood only by a few initiates or insiders. This gives the gospel the wrong reputation. God's Word becomes a book of riddles that may unlock the secret of the future—if we're clever enough to read the lines on the palm of world history. You'll get farther with the Bible than you will with an old woman in a shawl who gazes into a crystal ball or reads tea leaves.

If the political events of our time are to be used as confirmations and fulfillments of the Bible's prophecies, do we still need faith? More specifically, do we still need to believe in the *foolishness* of the cross?

Will Lindsey's view of the Bible win general acceptance throughout the churches? That would do the churches incalculable damage. Let's stop reading the Bible as a book of prophetic puzzles, puzzles to be solved by the human ingenuity. The Bible proclaims the *gospel*!

Hal Lindsey's good intentions do not make his views any less dangerous to the welfare of God's people. The main point is that his emphasis on puzzles and mysteries that have finally been unraveled in our time casts a false light on Scripture.

Pity those who look to Lindsey's books to lead them through the Bible. Lindsey's views represent yet another link in a long chain of mistaken interpretations of God's Word. And mistakes in this area can lead to definite harm. In the final analysis, Lindsey's reading of Scripture is a new form of Christian Gnosticism.

Israel and the Israelis

An important distinction

One of the great mistakes Hal Lindsey makes is confusing "Israel" (the covenant people referred to so often in the Bible) with the modern state of Israel. Unfortunately, he's not the only one who makes this cardinal error. This error has such drastic consequences in his case that we must give it our careful attention.

The reason Lindsey winds up confusing Israel and the Israelis is that he has no grasp of the *covenant*. Again, he's not the only one. But if he read Scripture more carefully, he would not make this mistake. The result of his error is that he applies every Bible text about the future of "Israel" to the Israelis and the modern state of Israel.

In Scripture, Israel is not just "the Jewish people" but the people of the *covenant*. Israel remained God's covenant people until He took away that privileged covenant status in the year 70. Even after Pentecost, the Lord continued to address Israel as the covenant people. Thus we must not assume that Israel's rights as the covenant people disappeared immediately after Golgotha.

In Acts 3:25, Peter says: "You *are* the sons of the prophets and of the covenant which God gave to your fathers." And Paul speaks of the Jews, his brothers according to the flesh, as follows: "They *are* Israelites, and to them belong the sonship, the glory, the covenants . . . to them belong the patriarchs" (Rom. 9:4-5). Later on Paul says: "They are enemies of God, for your sake; but as

56

regards election they are beloved for the sake of their forefathers" (Rom. 11:28).

We may not expand such statements to cover today's Jews, as many interpreters do. Paul speaks out of his own situation. What he said then does not authorize us to put the Jews of his day (to whom a covenantal appeal could still be addressed) on the same level as the Jews of our day. To do so would be to ignore the development of redemptive history.

In the period between Pentecost and the destruction of Jerusalem, Israel was still addressed as the covenant people. But there was a limit to that appeal, a limit imposed by God's impending judgment on His stubborn covenant people.

In Acts 3:22-3 Peter points to Deuteronomy 18:15, 18-19 and Leviticus 23:29. Anyone who does not listen to the prophet Jesus Christ will be completely cut off from among His people.

This is clear language. Peter is pointing to a boundary, a limit. If Israel refuses to listen to what the Spirit says through Jesus Christ, her covenant privileges will be taken away. Instead of being the covenant people, Israel will then be a mere nation, an *ethnos*. Only through the righteousness of faith can one become a child of Abraham and an heir to the promise (Rom. 4:13,16).

Hal Lindsey seems unaware of Israel's status as God's chosen people under the old covenant. Hence, the implications of this status for understanding the New Testament escape him, as well as the significance of God's judgment on Israel in the year 70. He neglects the Biblical emphases and simply reasons that when the Bible speaks of "Israel," it means the Jewish people. Thus, any text in the Bible about "Israel" can be applied to the Israelis.

The premises on which Lindsey constructs his argument are unsound. Therefore his conclusions are not reliable either. He comes to us with predictions about the future and even provides maps of future military operations. In

fact he's leading an army of snowmen who will quickly melt
in the intense sunlight of Scripture.

Why such interest in the Jews?

Hal Lindsey has his reasons for taking such an intense interest in the Jews. On page 32 of *The Late Great Planet
Earth* he asserts, without presenting any evidence: "Some
time in the future there will be a seven-year period climaxed
by the visible return of Jesus Christ."

What we face here is the old dispensationalist notion of
the seven-year kingdom. Lindsey arrived at the figure of
seven years by adding up the 42 months and 1260 days of
Revelation 11:2-3 (see PE, 33-4).

Lindsey claims that we are still living in the age of the
church. This age will end when the believers are taken up
to Christ. That event (the Rapture) will mark the beginning
of the seven-year period, a period in which the state of
Israel will play a major role and World War III will begin.
During that period, more people will turn to Christ in faith
(PE, 132). Through the work of 144,000 Jewish
evangelists, there will be a great revival among the Jews
(NW, 120-3).

Before that happens, however, the Jewish people will get
themselves into a situation that makes a dramatic change
necessary. That's the reason why Lindsey is so interested in
the development of the modern state of Israel.

A secularized interpretation of Israel's restoration

Lindsey likes to talk about the "rebirth" of Israel. By this
he means the return of the Jews to Palestine as their
homeland (see PE, 32). This perspective on Israel represents a colossal secularizing of the meaning of the Biblical
prophecies. We also find such secularizing among Chiliasts
of all sorts.

Ezekiel spoke of the restoration of "Israel," and his prophecy was fulfilled in the return of the "remnant" and later the establishment of the New Testament church. The covenant line was continued in that remnant and the church. But Lindsey calmly applies Ezekiel 38:8 to the settling of the Jews in Palestine: ". . . its *people* are brough forth out of the nations . . ." (PE, 40, where he quotes from Ezekiel). The vision of the dry bones in the valley (Ezek. 37) he applies to the "physical restoration" of the Jews and later to their "spiritual restoration," i.e. their conversion.

The establishment of the state of Israel in 1948 is not the only profoundly significant event, according to Lindsey. Also deeply meaningful is the conquest of Jerusalem in 1967. Signs of the times! But we still await a third sign—the rebuilding of the temple.

The rebuilding of the temple

Matthew 24:15 speaks of a "desolating sacrilege" in the "holy place" (i.e. the Herodian temple). Lindsey, however, chooses to read Matthew 24 as a prophecy that still awaits fulfillment. This assumption then becomes the basis for the next step in the argument: someday the temple will be rebuilt (PE, 45).

On the basis of the book of Revelation, he goes even further in his visions of the future. The Antichrist will establish his headquarters in *Rome*, but he will also enter the newly rebuilt Jewish temple and place a statue of himself in the Holy of Holies. He will proclaim himself to be God and demand that everyone worship him and his statue (NW, 178).

Now, the views Lindsey defends can be traced all the way back to certain church fathers. But that doesn't mean that his long story about the rebuilding of the Jewish temple and the Antichrist's desecration of the temple can be supported on Scriptural grounds.

Lindsey proceeds from a completely mistaken understanding of Scripture. He appeals to Matthew 24:34, where Jesus said that "this generation" would not pass away before all these things came to pass. He then reasons that a generation lasts about 40 years. Hence, within 40 years of 1948 (the date of the founding of the state of Israel), "all these things" will take place. He adds: "Many scholars who have studied Bible prophecy all their lives believe that this is so" (PE, 43).

It's remarkable that people who are so much in favor of a *literal* reading of the Bible will sometimes come up with a reading that's far from literal. Christ spoke of *"this* generation," using the same language He used in Matthew 16:28: "There are some standing here who will not taste death before they see the Son of man coming in his kingdom." In both cases He meant the *present* generation, that is, the people alive in His time.

When Christ spoke of the "desolating sacrilege," He was referring to future apostasy on the part of the *covenant people.* Wasn't the temple eventually used as a deified fortress during the Jewish rebellion against Rome?

The idea that we must await the rebuilding of the temple as one of the signs of the times can safely be dismissed. Even if a new temple were to be built by the Jews in Israel—and that's not likely, given the prevailing secular outlook there—this would not be a sign that any seven-year period and "Rapture" were just around the corner.

When Christ spoke of the "desolating sacrilege," He was giving His followers in Jerusalem an indication by which they would know when their mission among the covenant people had ended. Once the Jewish soldiers took over the "holy place," there would be nothing for the Christians to do but run for their lives.

In the light of Luke 21:20, we must read Christ's words in Matthew 24 as referring to a situation in which Jerusalem is surrounded by *Jewish* troops. When that happened, the disciples could still flee Jerusalem (Luke 21:21), for they would not be running into the arms of Roman soldiers.

The blossoming fig tree

Hal Lindsey also likes to appeal to Christ's words about the blossoming fig tree: "From the fig tree learn its lesson: as soon as its branch becomes tender and puts forth its leaves, you know that summer is near. So also, when you see all these things, you know that he is near, at the very gates" (Matt. 24:32-3). And he is not the only one who applies these words to the restoration of Israel since 1948.

But however many have made this mistake, it remains a mistake. Jesus was talking about events that would precede the destruction of Jerusalem. We have no right to give such a passage an interpretation of our own devising.

The return of Jesus Christ will be heralded by *one* sign only—the preaching of the gospel (Matt. 16:1-4). No other sign will be given than the sign of Jonah—the preaching of the crucified and risen Lord.

It's high time for Christians to realize that the church is a continuation of God's covenant people. This realization requires breaking with Jewish misconceptions, including the false belief that the restoration of the Jewish nation is a sign that the end is near.

The Lord accepts Jews into His church; He does so without reservation. But when they join God's church, they are *entering* the covenant. They were not in the covenant already while they were outside the church.

We must break with the idea that the modern nation of Israel is a quasi-church, a people for whom God somehow makes room in His covenant. We must likewise break with the notion that there is some sort of special future in store for the Jews.

Romans 11:28 does not provide any basis for such a belief. In this passage Paul is talking about Jews who were covenant children and accepted the gospel in his time (i.e. the period of roughly 40 years between Christ's ascension and the destruction of Jerusalem). In them "all Israel" was saved.

The unbelieving Jews of our time are not children of the covenant. For them there are no special covenant promises.

Beloved for the sake of their forefathers?

In Romans 11:28 we read: "As regards the gospel they are enemies of God, for your sake; but as regards election they are beloved for the sake of their forefathers." Doesn't this mean that all the Jews—whether they believe or not—still form one people enjoying a special relationship to the Lord because of the covenant with Abraham?

Again, this is an incorrect reading of Scripture. Where does it go wrong? It fails to take *redemptive history* into account.

The Jews to whom the first Christian church turned with the gospel were indeed "sons of the covenant" (Acts 3:25). But membership in the covenant is not something that is passed on to subsequent generations whether they believe or not. Grace is not something we inherit from our parents.

Many Christian churches have disappeared without a trace. Do we say to the descendants of the people who made up those churches: "You are sons of the covenant, and you are beloved for the sake of your forefathers"? Of course not! But when it comes to the Jews, that's exactly what many of us do, pointing to Romans 11 as our justification.

Let me repeat: Paul spoke out of the situation of his own time, the time of the interim, the time before the Lord settled accounts with the Jews via the destruction of the temple city of Jerusalem. Paul was fully justified in speaking of the Jews as "beloved for the sake of their forefathers." But in the face of nineteen centuries of stubborn refusal to recognize Jesus as the Messiah, we are not to do the same.

Unfortunately, even those who warn against the dangers of Hal Lindsey's reading of Scripture don't differ with him on Romans 11. We see this, for example, in George C. Miladin's analysis of Lindsey (*Is This Really the End? A Reformed Analysis of "The Late Great Planet Earth,"*

published by Mack Publishing Company of Cherry Hill,
N.J. in 1974). Miladin speaks of a great future promise
about the Jews (p. 12). He argues that the New Testament
teaches that there will be a spiritual revival of Israel
some day, as one of the signs that the end is near (p. 20).
Such statements bolster the dispensationalist cause. All the
same, Miladin does advance solid Scriptural arguments
against the dispensationalist position. Yet, the fact that he
clings to the idea of a future revival of Israel shows that on
this point he has nothing to say in response to Lindsey.

That's why it's so important to make it clear that when
Paul talks about the Jews in Romans 11, he means the Jews
of *his own time*. Included among the Jews were many
people who accepted the gospel. In this way the Lord was
fulfilling His promises. "All Israel" (i.e. the chosen among
Israel, as representatives of the people) was saved through
obedience to the gospel. By "all Israel," Paul meant the
remnant. He was appealing to the church in Rome not to
write Israel off: the apostate sons of the covenant were to be
called back to obedience.

But this is not to say that we are forced to regard the unbelieving Jews of *our time* as "sons of the covenant."
Neither should we conclude that the Biblical prophecies
about the restoration of Israel point to a mass conversion of
unbelieving Jews at the end of time. The acceptance of
these conclusions has done a great deal of harm in the
church and has made believers defenseless in the face of
Chiliastic and dispensationalist ideas.

Naturally, we must not manipulate Scripture in our efforts to show where Hal Lindsey's dispensationalism goes
wrong. But if our own exegesis has been on the wrong track
for a long time, we had better take a fresh look at our interpretation of key passages, before further damage is done.

The fact that certain prominent Christians also awaited a
mass conversion of the Jews should not influence our
thinking, for we base our beliefs on *Scripture*. The problem
with these Christian leaders is that they failed to read
Romans 11 from the proper redemptive historical perspec-

tive and failed to reckon with the covenant as the determining factor for weighing the status of the Jews. Since the errors of teachers are often magnified by their students, it is high time that we take a fresh look at the whole question.

Does Romans 11 support Hal Lindsey's position—yes or no? My conclusion is that this famous chapter does not support the neo-dispensationalist outlook in any way. Only when Romans 11 is torn out of its context can it serve as evidence for Lindsey's views. We all know the dangers of reading Bible passages out of context.

The Last Days

Hal Lindsey's calendar

When the rebuilding of the temple in Jerusalem is near, it will be time for the "Rapture." The believers will be taken up to Christ in the air, but the world will go right on turning and life will continue. Everywhere people will disappear suddenly—from athletic fields, from lecture halls, from offices, from churches. That's why we read on bumper stickers: "If the driver disappears, grab the wheel!"

After the Rapture, the seven-year period will begin. For 3 1/2 years, the two witnesses, whom Lindsey calls "Jesus freaks," will go about their work. After that the Antichrist will bare his fangs and the persecution (the Great Tribulation) will begin.

At about that time, the inferno of World War III will break out, with Jerusalem at the center of events. Once those seven frightening years are over, Jesus will return and the millennial kingdom will begin. That kingdom, in turn, will be followed by judgment and, finally, ultimate glory.

This, in brief, is Hal Lindsey's calendar. (I'll come back to the political details in a later chapter.) How are we to respond to such a vision of the last things?

For one thing, we should note that Lindsey admitted in a recent interview (*Eternity* magazine, January 1977, pp. 80-1) that his conception of the Rapture and the events following it is not based solely on Scriptural evidence. There is a *logical inference* involved: "As a premillennialist, I believe that when Christ returns there must be surviving, mortal believers to go into the millennium and repopulate the earth." Here we see what's really going on! To provide a population for the millennial kingdom, there have to be believers on earth *after* the Rapture. That's what logic dictates. But is the assumption about the coming millennium justified?

A critical appraisal

Throughout the history of the church, reflection on the last things has been a source of excitement. The official confessions of the Reformation, however, dealt with the last things in a sober way. Needless speculation was thereby discouraged. Although the Roman Catholics and Anabaptists could speak confidently of the events to occur at the end of the present dispensation, Calvin resolutely refused to deal with such questions at any length. He had seen too many evil consequences of such speculation in the circles of the Anabaptists and other sectarians.

Later generations were less hesitant. Since the rise of pietism, Chiliasm has reared its ugly head again, with the result that speculation about the last days is now regarded as legitimate.

People began to ask whether the church's official standpoint on such matters as the so-called Rapture and the millennial kingdom is Scripturally justifiable. Could it be that pietists and others have made so much of these doctrines because they did not get proper attention in official church circles?

Scripture does speak of a "Rapture," a time when the believers are taken up to meet Christ in the air (I Thess. 4:13-18). But the Bible does not say anything about a millennial kingdom *on the earth*. Is the Augustinian interpretation, namely, that the millennium is simply the period between Christ's ascension and His return, correct?

It seems to me that the thousand-year period mentioned

in Revelation 20 is to be read as a prophecy about the day of the Lord, the day that begins when the believers are taken up to meet Christ. Moreover, we should bear in mind that the dominant Augustinian interpretation was not accepted in the confessions. During the time of the Reformation, there were many who believed that the thousand-year period was already over.

To get a better grasp of Hal Lindsey's views on the last things, bear in mind the following four theses he defends: (1) Christ's return will not occur at the same time as the Rapture, the day when the believers are taken up to heaven. (2) After the Rapture there will be a seven-year period during which people will still be able to repent and turn to Christ. (3) During that seven-year period, many of the Biblical prophecies will be fulfilled. (4) The Jews will play a major role in the seven-year period.

These four points cannot be defended on Scriptural grounds. Let's look at them one by one.

(1) According to I Thessalonians 4, the believers will be taken up to *meet Christ* as He returns. Thus we may not separate the "Rapture" from Christ's return.

(2) There is no seven-year period following the "Rapture." The idea of such a period is based on an arbitrary reading of Revelation 11:2-3. Moreover, Scripture says nothing about any opportunity for repentance and conversion *after* Christ's return.

(3) It's typical of sectarian thinking that all sorts of prophecies are supposed to be fulfilled during the seven-year period. Sectarians seek a temporal framework within which they can place sensational events. This means that a special period must be created. They don't seem to realize that those Old Testament prophecies that they hope to see fulfilled in the seven-year period have already been fulfilled.

(4) The claim that we now live in the age of the *church* and that there will be another period in which the Jews play a dominant role is completely in conflict with the function the Lord has assigned to the church as the body of

believers. The special period is created to make room for the realization of age-old Jewish dreams.

Thus Hal Lindsey's vision of the last things is to be rejected. It is in conflict with the confessions of the Reformation, which do not teach that the Jewish people and the city of Jerusalem will be dominant at the end of time. Lindsey's thought represents a form of eschatologized Judaism.

The book of Revelation and the seven-year period

Lindsey claims that the church is mentioned nineteen times in the first three chapters of the book of Revelation but is never once spoken of in chapters 4-19 as being *on the earth*. In chapters 2 and 3 we read repeatedly: "He who has an ear, let him hear what the Spirit says to the *churches*." In Revelation 13:9 we read: "If any one has an ear, let him hear." The words "what the Spirit says to the churches" are left out. It is inconceivable, Lindsey argues, that God would fail to mention the church if it was still on earth during the time of the judgments described in the book of Revelation.

According to Lindsey, Christ's reference to the times of Noah and Lot (Matt. 24) indicates that the church will be taken up to heaven *before* the Tribulation (NW, 78-80). Thus the Rapture will take place before the events described in Revelation 4.

Now, if this were really true, we would have to change our thinking dramatically. A Copernican revolution would be in order, and we would have to rewrite our commentaries on the book of Revelation.

Hal Lindsey and the seven churches

No proper assessment of Lindsey's outlook on the last things is possible without an analysis of his view of the seven churches in the book of Revelation (see NW, 38ff). In this area, too, his views are not new; he takes over ideas developed by Franciscan mystics before the Reformation and later accepted by Cocceius and certain pietists. The seven churches, he tells us, represent the *seven ages of the church.*

Now, adherents of this view do not always agree. History marches on, and it becomes necessary to draw up new divisions of the seven ages every now and then. Hence the disagreements.

Lindsey offers the following division of church history, which can be compared with the divisions made by Cocceius (1603-69) and Campegius Vitringa (1659-1722).

	Lindsey	Cocceius	Vitringa
Ephesus:	apostolic church	same as Lindsey	church of 90-250
Smyrna:	the church persecuted by the Roman emperors	same as Lindsey	church of 250-313
Pergagum:	church of 312-590	same as Lindsey	church of 270 to the end of the 7th century
Thyatira:	church of 590-1517	same as Lindsey	church from the end of the 7th century to 1200
Sardis:	church of 1517-1750	church of the Reformation era	church of 1200-1500
Philadelphia:	church of 1750-1925	the Reformed church	church since the Reformation era
Laodicea:	church of 1900 to the Tribulation	church of the last days	final state of the church

According to Lindsey, Revelation 2 and 3 present the history of the church before the Rapture, while chapters 4-19 describe the period after the Rapture. But is this interpretation of the messages to the seven churches correct? Are the seven messages a survey of church history?

What about those seven churches?

The book of Revelation is addressed to seven churches—that much we are told (Rev. 1:4). Now, wouldn't it be best to accept this as a simple fact instead of looking for some mysterious "truth behind the truth"? Who gives us the right to decide that this book is really intended as a characterization of the "seven ages of the church"? There is nothing in the book of Revelation to justify such a view. Moreover, the contrast between Lindsey and Cocceius shows that this scheme must be reworked periodically because of the passage of time. Allegorical tricks become necessary to support such readings of Scripture.

The views held by the followers of the famous medieval abbot Joachim of Fiore are again brought into play in Lindsey's books. Let's not forget that Joachim was waiting for the age of the Spirit as the climax of history. His scheme about the seven ages of the church is especially dangerous for our day, when the charismatic movement is gaining ground so rapidly.

Time and again I am struck by the great liberties Lindsey takes with Scripture. I cannot help wondering: Doesn't he know anything about hermeneutics, about the principles used to interpret Scripture? Who gave him the right to turn the Revelation to John into a mysterious book with a hidden meaning?

The book of Revelation presents a clear testimony to the churches in the *first* century. To be more specific, I am convinced that Revelation was written in the seventh decade of the first century—*before* the destruction of Jerusalem in the year 70, which Jesus talked about in Mattew 24.

Once the theory of the seven ages of the church is disposed of, it becomes clear that Lindsey has no grounds for his thesis that Revelation 4-19 deals with the time after the so-called Rapture. Moreover, we must not simply take Lindsey's word for it that there is nothing said about the church on earth in these chapters.

The church in Revelation 4-19

The book of Revelation opens with an introduction. Then come the seven messages. The material following the seven messages, however, is not a new beginning but a continuation, a clarification, a deepening.

We are all familiar with books containing illustrations in cartoon style. Think of the theology of "Peanuts." There is even a Christian Reformed study book dealing with the Heidelberg Catechism that contains cartoons.

Likewise the book of Revelation. As we saw in Chapter 2, the material that begins with Revelation 4 can be read as a series of cartoons illustrating the book's central message.

Sounds sacriligious? Maybe, but it's hardly a new insight. A book by Albertus Pieters published in 1937 already speaks of the Revelation to John as "God's Picture Book" (*The Lamb, the Woman and the Dragon,* published by Eerdmans, p. 34). In that book the visions of John are compared with political cartoons. There is even a cartoon reproduced in the book for purposes of comparison (opposite p. 36).

Thus there is precedent for the thesis that what we find in Revelation 4 illustrates the message presented earlier to the churches—in a strikingly modern way, at that! I don't mean to deny that new, further revelation is presented in the chapters that come after the "seven letters"; the point I wish to emphasize is simply that these chapters *clarify* and *illustrate* what comes before. Thus they are addressed to the church on earth, just as the seven letters are.

When these seven messages from the King are carefully

compared with the rest of the book of Revelation, we see how closely the two parts of the last book of the Bible hang together. I will list only a few examples; there are many more I could mention. And for the present, I will ignore the last three chapters of Revelation.

Revelation 2-3		Revelation 4-19
2:2, 19	perseverance	13:10
2:2	labor, toil	14:13
2:7	those who conquer	15:2
2:9	slander	13:5-6
2:9, 13, 24	satan	12:9
2:10	faithful	17:14
2:13	throne of satan	13:2
2:16	sword of Christ's mouth	19:15, 21
2:14, 20	false prophecy	16:13
2:20ff	fornication	9:21; 17:2ff; 18:3ff
2:22	repentance	16:11
2:27	rod of iron	12:5; 19:15
3:2	stay awake	16:15
3:3	come like a thief	16:15
3:5	white garments	6:11; 7:9, 13; 19:8
3:5	book of life	5:1ff; 13:8; 17:8
3:8	open door	4:1
3:10	the whole world	16:14
3:10	inhabitants of the earth	13:12, 14
3:12	temple of God	7:15; 11:1, 19
3:18	nakedness	16:15
3:20	a meal	19:9
3:21	throne of God	4:2-6, 9

The fact that the same kind of language and images are used in Revelation 4-19 as in Revelation 2-3 indicates that the visions are meant for the same group as the "messages"—the church on earth in those days and also the church of later ages, including today's church. The visions shed light on the seven messages.

Let's look more closely at the question whether Revelation 4-19 ignores the church on earth. In 5:3 we read that no one *on earth* was worthy to open the scroll. In 5:13 we hear every creature in heaven and *on earth* singing praises. Doesn't that include people? Shouldn't we read this text as a reference to the church's liturgy? We are shown that the church on earth *before* the Rapture is drawn into Christ's redemptive work.

As we read on, we come across references to the prayers of the saints (5:8; 8:3-4). Who gives us the right to decide that only the prayers of believers *after* the Rapture are meant here? Were the initial readers of the book of Revelation supposed to assume that such texts had nothing to do with *their* prayers, that they referred only to believers on the earth *after* the Rapture.

Once more I must ask: How could the initial circle of readers ever come up with such an interpretation? Can Lindsey cite as much as one example of this interpretation in the patristic literature of the early Christian church?

In Revelation 6 we read about judgments. The background of that chapter is not just Matthew 24 but also Leviticus 26 and Deuteronomy 28, where we read about the *covenant wrath* to be poured down on the covenant people if they are unfaithful and go astray.

The book of Revelation picks up this Old Testament theme of covenant wrath and warns that the Lord will not forever delay His coming in judgment. That judgment will strike those among the covenant people who do not repent and recognize Jesus Christ as the Messiah. The church has good reason to be on guard. If the church goes astray, she will be subject to the same covenant wrath. Think of the seven messages to the churches!

The issue in Revelation 6:6-11 is clearly the church in her struggle on earth before the Rapture. John talks about those who were slain for the sake of God's Word and tells us that they cry out for revenge. He also speaks of brothers who are still to be put to death. Are we now to assume that the first readers were expected to read such passages with the aid of a telescope or a pair of binoculars, keeping their eyes fixed on the believers who would be put to death *after* the Rapture?

This passage in Revelation must be read in the light of what Christ says in Luke 21:16: "Some of you, they will put to death." Or does Lindsey mean to say that even this text should be applied to the period that comes after the so-called Rapture?

What Revelation 11-13 describes is an attack on the church on earth. Again, there is no basis for assuming, as Lindsey does, that this attack on the believers is to occur *after* the Rapture. Why shouldn't the appeals for persever-ance (13:10, 18; 16:15) apply to the church on earth before Christ's return? And what about the dead who "die in the Lord" (14:13). Does that text apply *only* to believers who die after the Rapture? According to Lindsey, it does: "When John mentions the perseverance of the saints, he's speaking of the Tribulation believers who will die for Christ rather than receive the mark of Satan's tyrant, the An-tichrist" (NW, 203).

Once more I must ask: Wasn't this text (Rev. 14:13) in-tended first of all for the original readers of the Revelation to John? Or was John expecting them to say to themselves: "That only applies to the 'Tribulation believers' in the twentieth century"?

Let's look at another text: "Come out of her, my people" (18:4). What gives Lindsey the right to transform this ap-peal to leave Babylon into a reference to a wicked city in the "end time" after the Rapture? Such an interpretation would mean that the text had nothing to say to its original readers.

"My people," that is, God's covenant people (Greek: *laos*), are being addressed here. Doesn't the New Testament church in the "church age" count as part of the covenant people? Surely Lindsey doesn't propose to limit "my [covenant] people" to the believers after the Rapture!

Lindsey apparently assumed that the first readers of Revelation were a distantiated group not personally involved in the struggles depicted in the book. Apparently these poor people had nothing better to do with their time than gaze into the future with their telescopes.

This illustrates once more that Lindsey has no real grasp of the *unity* of the book of Revelation. In fact, the unity of Scriptural revelation as a whole escapes him as well. The name *Babylon* as it occurs in Revelation is not just to be viewed as a prophetic term for some *future* power. The exegesis of Revelation is bound to go astray if we insist on viewing the book as a collection of prophecies about the future.

Revelation 17-18 must be read in the light of Matthew 23-24. These chapters do not speak first of all about events that are finally taking place in our time or are still to come; they speak of the city that kills the prophets! The original readers were being informed about the coming fall of the city of the covenant; they were being told to forsake that city.

At hand was the time of covenant judgment, the time of judgment on those whose hands were stained with the blood of Jesus, Stephen and James. The "desolating sacrilege" was not far away. Hence the appeal: "Come out of her, my people." The church on earth is addressed in this appeal, for Babylon was surely not a power that would appear on the scene after the Rapture.

The Great Tribulation

Three and a half years after the Rapture comes the Tribulation, the time of great oppression. This is an axiom for Hal Lindsey. The talk of Babylon and the Beast fits into this period.

This axiom, too, must be rejected. It is thoroughly unscriptural.

The first place in the New Testament where we read about a "great tribulation" is Matthew 24:21. In the immediately preceding verses, we read an appeal to flee

Jerusalem when the sign of the "desolating sacrilege" is given. Why must the believers flee? "For then there will be great tribulation such as has not been from the beginning of the world until now, no, and *never will be*." We read similar language in Daniel 12:1: "And there shall be a time of trouble, such as never has been." The text does not go on and say: "and never will be again."

We must take this difference between the two passages into account. The time Jesus spoke of was the perilous hour before the destruction of Jerusalem. That hour lay in the future for Daniel. It also lay in the future for Jesus, but Jesus knew that the church would live beyond that period! That's why He added that there will never be such a time again.

In Revelation 7:14 we are also told about "great tribulation." What is to prevent us from reading this text in the light of Matthew 24:21? Wasn't the church indeed saved in an hour of extreme peril?

Only when we insist on reading Matthew 24 in the light of a telescope theology are we forced to conclude that Jesus was talking about something other than the destruction of Jerusalem. Lindsey places the "desolating sacrilege" not in an Herodian temple of Jesus' time but in a rebuilt temple after the Rapture. The Great Tribulation is likewise scheduled for the time after the Rapture.

How does Lindsey reach such a conclusion? Presumably he reasons as follows. The talk of "great tribulation" could not apply only to the time before the destruction of Jerusalem, for there was even worse tribulation for the believers under various emperors and popes—to say nothing of the coming persecution by the Antichrist. Therefore, when Christ talked about "great tribulation," He must have meant something that lay in the future, beyond the Rapture.

The usual interpretation of Matthew 24 helps to further this view of the last things. Lindsey clings stubbornly to the axiom that Jesus, in Matthew 24, was talking to His disciples about events far in the future, events that still have not occurred. Like so many others, Lindsey seems blind to the possibility that the judgment Jesus sent on Jerusalem is to be regarded as a "coming" on His part (to deliver His people and to strike His enemies with covenant wrath).

In an interview in *Eternity* magazine (January 1977), Lindsey argued: "If the rapture occurs at the end of the tribulation, then all of these passages about the sudden mysterious coming of Christ—people will not be aware, one will be taken of two people working in the field—none of this makes sense." He points to Jesus' use of Noah's time as an illustration—people eating, drinking, marrying, planting, building, and so forth. "There's no way to conduct those normal activities at the end of the tribulation. Half the population of the world will have been wiped out." (p. 81).

Here one circular argument becomes the basis for another, as formal logic triumphs over exegesis. Matthew 24 is squeezed until it gives us "prophecy" about our time.

And so the Tribulation axiom lives on. Even on the basis of historical data it is argued that Jesus could not have been referring to the time before the destruction of Jerusalem. The urge to create an apocalyptic calendar is so strong that people are no longer willing to recognize and honor the original meaning of Matthew 24 and parallel passages. The way is open for the Tribulation bogeyman that haunts so many Christians in their outlook on the future.

As the Tribulation theme is worked out, the rule of thumb seems to be: the zanier, the better. The result is fiction, speculation.

In the next chapter we will see which political events Hal Lindsey awaits in the seven-year Tribulation period.

Hal Lindsey's Political Almanac

"Goggology"

Russia = Gog—that's another of Hal Lindsey's axioms. The proof? Ezekiel 38-9, Daniel 11:40-5, and Joel 2:20. The "Rosh" referred to in Ezekiel 38:2 (in some translations) is Russia, while Meshech is Moscow (PE, 48ff). After all, Russia is to the north of Israel, and Gog's army is described as very strong.

Russia has many allies in Africa and Asia. This fits in nicely with what we read in Ezekiel 38 about the Ethiopians (Cush) and the Libyans as allies. "Gomer" is then a reference to Russia's satellites behind the Iron Curtain. "Beth-togarmah" is a reference to the Cossacks and other people in the eastern part of Russia. Aren't all these people armed with weapons produced by the Russians? (PE, 56ff). It all falls neatly into place in Lindsey's "Goggology"!

The method of exegesis that Lindsey applies here is not new. It has been used extensively by the Chiliasts as well as the spokesmen of the British Israel movement. In 1940 a little book was published in England under the title *Armageddon Is at the Doors*. Its author, A. J. Ferris, spoke of the final struggle for control of the world, a struggle that would pit the Russian Communist block against Israel and the Anglo-Saxon nations. (The British Israel movement maintains that the tribes of Ephraim and Manasseh lived on in the Anglo-Saxon race.)

In the light of this outlook, Ezekiel 38-39 is read as

predicting an Armageddon in which Russia clashes with British Israel. Like Lindsey, Ferris identifies Rosh with Russia, Meshech with Moscow, and Tubal with Tobolsk. It's all part of "Goggological" dogmatics!

What are we to make of such identifications? It is striking that when Revelation 20 speaks of Gog and Magog, Lindsey says only that they are among the descendants of Israel's enemies (Gog and Magog) born during the time of the millennium (NW, 278). Here the name *Rosh* is not mentioned, and the concept "enemies of Israel" is still fairly broad.

Moreover, Lindsey's neglect of the concept of the covenant is also apparent here. He speaks of enemies of "Israel," pointing to the modern state of Israel, whereas the reference is really to enemies of Israel as the covenant people, the church. That he does not speak of Russians in connection with Revelation 20 but uses a more general term should not escape our attention either.

In Ezekiel 38-39, we are told about an overpowering attack made on the land of Israel. Yet the enemy forces are destroyed. Then come the visions about the new city and the temple (Ezek. 40-48; see also the book of Revelation). This material is to be read as visionary prophecy. Some scholars looking for a fulfillment of this prophecy have pointed to an attack on Palestine by the Scythians, and others to the career of Antiochus Epiphanes. Other attacks on the church, including the threat described in Revelation 20 in connection with the day of the Lord, can also be regarded as fulfillments of the Gog episode. Therefore it is foolish to use Ezekiel 38-39 as a source of political predictions about the so-called Tribulation period after the Rapture.

Such use of Bible texts is inconsistent and arbitrary. In the Old Testament we read prophecies about various people—the Ammonites, the Moabites, the Edomites, and so forth. Why doesn't Lindsey make much of them too? Probably because they have disappeared in the general mingling of nations and races in the ancient Near East.

But if the Moabites have disappeared, how can Lindsey be so sure that today's Russians are pure descendants of the peoples mentioned in Ezekiel 38? It's no more true than the misconception that the Jews in the world today are pure descendants of Abraham. In fact, the Jews in eastern Europe have a lot of Russian blood running through their veins—which is what makes the whole situation more complicated and Lindsey's standpoint even more ridiculous. Entire Russian tribes that were converted to Judaism in the Middle Ages now live on in the Jewish population of eastern Europe.

It is well known that many Jews were involved in the rise and development of Communism. Anyone who visits Israel can see for himself how much Communist literature there is in the kibbutz libraries. If we were to follow Lindsey's method of reasoning, we could say that there is a heavy dose of Gog's blood running through the views of today's Jews. We could oppose Lindsey with his own weapons by declaring: Israel = Gog.

There is even a measure of truth to this, for what Ezekiel 38 and 39 present us with in typological fashion is opposition to the gospel. This comes out in both Communism and the Jewish rejection of Christ.

The proposition "Russia = Gog" is also unfair because there are so many Christians living in Russia. The political mirages with which Lindsey presents us are so bizarre that they would hardly arouse our curiosity if they were not accepted as gospel by hundreds of thousands of people.

The basic mistakes made by Lindsey have their effect in every part of his vision of the future. He regards prophecy as *prediction* and then proceeds to present an almost completely literal interpretation of the "predictions." Because he ignores the *covenant* and the covenantal purpose of the messages of the prophets, it does not occur to him that a name like *Gog* might have a *typological* meaning.

Lindsey loves the chronological framework of the seven-year period after the Rapture plus the thousand-year kingdom of peace on earth to follow it. This framework leaves plenty of room for exegesis in which fantasy plays a prominent role—instead of an understanding of prophecy against the background of God's covenant relationship with Israel.

A political calendar covering seven years

Let's take a closer look at the developments Lindsey schedules for the seven years after the Rapture. For the first three and a half years of the seven-year Tribulation period, satan will rule the world through a Jewish Antichrist in Rome. This ruler will give the Jews permission to rebuild the temple. With this event, the seven-year period of Tribulation will begin officially (NW, 178). The rider on the white horse mentioned in Revelation 6 is the Antichrist. Lindsey believes that this European Antichrist is already alive and waiting his turn (NW, 103). The Antichrist, as the Beast, will be accompanied by a Jewish false prophet.

While these things are happening, the Jews will be converted in great numbers. This will in turn lead to a worldwide evangelism program undertaken by 144,000 Jewish evangelists.

After three and a half years, the Antichrist will show his true colors. In the Jewish temple in Jerusalem he will set up an image of himself. Immediately afterward, the peace in his empire will be shattered, for the red horse will be let loose—Russia and her allies (NW, 104). World War III will break out. Egypt will undertake an invasion of Israel, backed by her African and Asian allies. Russia will seize the opportunity to invade the Middle East, reaching out to seize Israel and its wealth by way of an amphibious and land invasion (PE, 142ff). This Lindsey derives from Daniel 11:40-1 and Ezekiel 38:14-16.

Even Egypt will be trampled underfoot by the Russians, according to Daniel 11:42-3. But the very next verse goes on to speak of rumors from the east and north that will scare the Russian invaders. This Lindsey interprets as a mobilization in the Far East and in Europe. The Russians will then withdraw from Egypt to consolidate their position in Israel.

In the meantime, the Roman dictator will begin an invasion of Israel. As for the mobilizations in the Far East, Lindsey assumes that the Red Chinese are meant (PE, 147). According to Revelation 9:14-16, an army of 200,000,000 Red Chinese will be on the march.

The Russians will set up their headquarters in the temple area of Jerusalem. But their awesome power will not deliver them (Dan. 11:45), for they will meet their Waterloo (Ezek. 38:18-22; 39:3-5). What Ezekiel says about fire and brimstone must be read as a reference to tactical nuclear weapons used against the Russians by the Roman dictator.

God will see to it that this barbarian Red Army suffers a total defeat. When Ezekiel declares that the armies of Gog will be completely destroyed (Ezek. 39), he is referring to the Russian Red Army (PE, 149-50). Russia itself will fall victim to nuclear weapons (Ezek. 39:6). The country that was once safe under the protection of the Antichrist will be struck by his wrath in the form of ballistic missiles. Lindsey regards it as possible that God will eventually intervene to punish Russia directly (PE, 150).

After the collapse of Russia, the Red Chinese will appear on the scene. They will cross the Euphrates and march on Palestine. The spearhead of the attack will be against the Roman dictator and his allies.

At last the final battle of the nations at Armageddon will begin, the battle in the Valley of Decision (Joel 3:9-14). The result will be worldwide destruction.

Only then will Jesus Christ appear with all the saints. When the Bible talks about Christ's coming on the "clouds," it means clouds or myriads of believers in white garments surrounding Him (PE, 162). These believers are the ones who were taken up to Him before the Tribulation began, including the risen saints of Old Testament times (Rev. 19:14).

That glorious return will inaugurate the millennium, the

thousand-year kingdom on earth. At the end of that period will come the final judgment, the new heaven and the new earth.

Jewish fables

Hal Lindsey rejects higher criticism of the Bible. Yet his own pseudo-hermeneutic leads to a fundamentally false understanding of Scripture. Lindsey turns the Bible into a political almanac. For him, to search the Scriptures is to engage in a treasure hunt for texts containing predictions. Those texts enable us to calculate what will come next in the arena of politics and international relations.

In this misuse of Scripture we see a modern form of Jewish apocalypticism such as first reared its head around the time of Christ. (Think of such writings as the book of Enoch, IV Ezra, and so forth.) This apocalypticism was often inspired by the nationalistic thinking of the Zealots, who believed that the Jews would again play a major role in world events and that the kingdoms of this world would be destroyed.

Christ was clearly opposed to such an understanding of the kingdom of God (see Matt. 16:1-4; 24:4-5, 23-4; Luke 17:20). The kingdom would not come in a way that could be calculated in advance. See to it that you are not misled on this point, He warned.

Hal Lindsey's misconceptions illustrate how Jewish dreams sometimes infiltrate Christian thinking. Such dreams are a temptation that we must resist.

A hermeneutical misunderstanding

Misconceptions about Biblical prophecy lead to misunderstandings in the area of exegesis. When Daniel 12 talks about the "time of the end" (vs. 4 and 9), some translations and interpretations turn this into the "end time." This in turn fosters the notions that Daniel's visions deal with the absolute end of history. Thus his prophecies are read not as pointing to events in the days of Antiochus Epiphanes, who ruled 175-164 B.C., but as portraying events at the very end of time. The expression "the last days," which is used by some of the other prophets, has furthered the same misconception.

What this led to was that prophecies such as Daniel 11 were no longer applied first of all to the time of the Seleucids and the Ptolemies. No, the fulfillment was awaited in the "end time," which still lies ahead of us. Ezekiel 38-39 and many other passages were likewise set adrift from their prophetic moorings, to be fulfilled in some vague, distant future.

It is not to be denied that many prophecies admit of more than one fulfillment. Hence the fulfillment is not completely bound to the nation or people named in the prophecy; there is a wider principle at stake. In Christ's prophecy recorded in Matthew 24, the desolating sacrilege mentioned by Daniel in his prophecy about the time of Antiochus Epiphanes (Dan. 9:27) becomes a reference to the manifest apostasy of the Jewish covenant people. And in the book of Revelation, Babylon becomes a type standing for Jewish unfaithfulness to the covenant.

What Lindsey and many others of the same persuasion fail to take into account is the historical perspective one must bring to the reading of Scripture. That's why they stubbornly overlook the initial fulfillments of the prophecies and argue for a fulfillment in a special dispensation to follow the Rapture. Perhaps we could speak of a post-Rapture complex in Lindsey's hermeneutics. As a result of this complex, all sorts of ancient prophecies about nations that have disappeared must be modernized, right down to the weaponry used in warfare.

If only Lindsey and others could get beyond this hermeneutical misunderstanding, their eyes would be opened to many things that they now fail to see. But as long as the dispensationalist notes in the *Scofield Reference Bible* retain their authority in the eyes of many Christians, this is not likely to happen.

On the basis of current political developments, I don't propose to argue against Lindsey's fantasies about the future. That would amount to falling into the same trap in which he himself is caught. The newspaper is not our guide to the Bible. Suffice it to say that Scripture itself becomes the martyr when we go so far astray in our exegesis. My hope and prayer is that this diagnosis will help heal some people of their Lindseyitis.

Where are the believers during the Great Tribulation?

The question could well be asked what becomes of the believers in Palestine during the cataclysmic upheavals in the Middle East. Hal Lindsey presents us with an amazing, original answer. When Revelation 12 speaks of "the two wings of the great eagle" that are given to the woman, it is talking about the Jewish believers in Palestine, who will be transported to a safe place in the wilderness, perhaps the natural fortress of Petra. A massive airlift will bring the Jewish believers over there. Because the eagle is a national symbol of the United States, it is possible that this airlift will be the work of airplanes of the American Sixth Fleet in the Mediterranean Sea (NW, 179).

Why is Lindsey so sure that the symbol of the eagle points to the United States? Why not West Germany? Or the Dutch cities of Nijmegen and Groningen, which also include the eagle on their coat of arms?

I had to read and reread this passage many times before I could bring myself to believe that Lindsey was serious. Now that I'm finally convinced, I present it as a typical example of his style of exegesis. When we read about the wings of the eagle in Exodus 19:4, where the theme of the entire Penteteuch is recorded, or in the song of Moses (Deut. 32: 11-12), are we also supposed to think in terms of American airplanes? Revelation 12:14 clearly points back to these passages in the Penteteuch.

Lindsey does not keep covenant motifs in mind in his reading of Scripture. He doesn't have time for them in his furious scramble for predictions in the Bible. Unfortunately, many Christians run after him, gobbling up his dispensationalism like candy.

Revelation 12 refers to the protection that Christ has promised His own in such passages as Matthew 24. That promise also belongs to us as the church of the twentieth century. By applying such a promise to an airlift in an imagined seven-year dispensation in which there is no church on earth, Lindsey robs today's church of the comfort of this promise. Sensationalism and speculation to satisfy our curiosity about the future take the place of the believer's assurance of faith.

Work to Be Done

We may not remain spectators

In earlier days, dispensationalist apocalypticism lived more or less outside the boundaries of the traditional church. That was understandable. Dispensationalism originated in sectarian circles where the church was out of favor. But now it is gaining a foothold with the church, just as the charismatic movement is doing.

Who will give us guidance in this area? Commentaries on the book of Revelation? If the authors of such commentaries want to have their work accepted as scholarly, they deal only with the doctrine of the millennial kingdom—and sometimes even defend it! For the rest they ignore the doctrines of the sectarians, including dispensationalism, as unscholarly and therefore not worthy of attention.

Am I my dispensationalist brother's keeper? The authors of the commentaries, apparently, say no. Sometimes Biblical scholars seem to assume that there is a gap between orthodoxy and scholarship, and that the concerns of orthodox, Bible-believing Christians challenged by sectarianism have nothing to do with Biblical scholarship.

In our day, the boundaries between "churches" and "sects" are eroding. The mass media play a role in this process. Thanks to popular dispensationalist journalism, broad sectors of the church's membership are being influenced as never before. That's why we may not remain mere spectators in the battle about the interpretation of Biblical prophecy and its application to our time. It is simply not enough to reject dispensationalism. We must be able to explain where it goes wrong and what the Bible does indeed intend to teach about the "last things."

Why is dispensationalist apocalypticism growing so rapidly?

If we wish to oppose the revolution wrought by apocalypticism, we must begin with some intensive research. Why is this caricature of Christian hope blossoming in our time?

First of all, we must recognize that not just young people but Christians of all ages are fed up with churches that preach little more than middle-class values, churches that conceal a great deal of uncertainty and uneasiness behind the inertia with which they resist change. The people in such churches are ripe for "something new." And there's plenty to choose from—charismatic and apocalyptic movements of all sorts. Since we live in a democratic age, an age in which all knowledge has to be packaged in some simple "Reader's Digest" style, they fail to recognize what superficial methods of Scriptural interpretation the dispensationalists are using. (The churches they attend aren't much better in this respect.) In place of the cold formalism of dying churches, they seek warmth, excitement, emotion, commitment.

In the second place, the superficiality of church life plays into the hands of the dispensationalist revolution. Many of today's preachers are more interested in sociology than the Bible. Their sermons are full of commentary on ethical, political and ecological issues. These preachers are paid counselors and entertainers. Their sermons become weaker and weaker in exegetical content and Scriptural insight.

The time when every preacher had a classical education is long gone. Not many of today's preachers are experts in theological scholarship and the languages of the Bible. For them the Bible is a source of slogans, texts to hang on the wall. And their favorite texts are not "spiritual" and "edifying" passages but passages that reflect social concerns.

As a result of these developments, the church's doctrines are neglected. Preaching must be up-to-date; each sermon must contain something "new," something "relevant." Scripture becomes a source of examples, allegories, mottoes. Such superficial theology turns the Bible's message inside out; the Bible becomes a source book of quotations to support "modern" views on various issues.

The weakness in the preaching in many churches definitely plays into the hands of the dispensationalists. A covenantal, redemptive historical approach to the Bible is rarely to be found. The confessions of the church are largely ignored, for doctrine is "irrelevant."

What about church members who still want to take the Bible seriously, who still take the trouble to search the Scriptures? Does the church give them the equipment they need? Do they have enough knowledge of the Scriptures to undertake the great task? All too often, they don't. Their earnestness is not matched by their insight.

When they come into contact with some movement that appeals constantly to the Bible, they are defenseless. The earnestness they encounter matches their own, and they are drawn in, believing they have "found" something. Only then do they sense just how dissatisfied they were with the wavering and uncertainty of their former church. Now the Bible is no longer a collection of loosely related texts for them; it is a closed system. They finally have peace in their hearts and something to hang on to, for they do not realize how fundamentally false their new-found system is.

1970 was an important year. Hal Lindsey published *The Late Great Planet Earth*. Salem Kirban's book *I Predict* also appeared that year. Another significant title appeared in Germany—Klaus Koch's *Ratlos vor der Apokalyptik* (Perplexed by Apocalypticism). Koch pointed out that Christian theology has left little or no room for eschatology. That there was a fear of apocalypticism in Europe is illustrated by the fact that there are so few scholarly commentaries on Daniel and Revelation.

Koch was right: prophecy of the sort found in Daniel and Revelation is widely regarded as mysterious territory to be avoided or left to the sectarians and other extremists. Liberal and horizontal theologies don't know what to do with Biblical apocalypticism. How would one demythologize the book of Revelation?

I suppose we are all somewhat guilty on that score. Many a preacher and professor has admitted in an honest moment that the Revelation to John is so difficult that he hardly knew where to start with it. The fear of sectarian speculation scares them off. "Let's not even deal with such subjects, for we simply don't know where we will wind up." The "letters" early in the book of Revelation might be discussed, as well as selected visions (e.g. the four horsemen, or the Beast). But that's where it ends.

In the Dutch Reformed circles from which I stem, there has not been a major scholarly commentary published on the book of Revelation since 1925. The last one was by Prof. S. Greijdanus and is actually an elaboration of a book written on a more popular level and published in 1908.

However deserving Greijdanus may be of praise—he knew Greek as few have ever known it—we should not canonize him. In his interpretation of the book of Revelation, he followed the usual method of applying the prophecies and visions to political and cultural events rather than interpreting the book in covenantal terms against the background of the Old Testament.

The assumption that Biblical "apocalypticism" deals with the same themes as Jewish apocalypticism was accepted by Greijdanus and applied in his commentary. As a result, he left room for sectarian speculation—although that was by no means his intention.

I must list a couple of examples, for there is a great deal at stake here. When Revelation 9 speaks of harnessed horses with fire and sulphur issuing from their mouths, Greijdanus comments:

The image of the horse is here intended to stand for the

weaponry of war. In this vision it symbolizes artillery, cannons, machine guns, and other horrible instruments of battle, in whatever form and structure they may exist or may be created in future. What we see described here is the operation of gunpowder, dynamite, poisonous gases, and so forth (p. 209).

Greijdanus clearly views this vision as a description of a general judgment to strike the whole world. He adds some color by referring to the weapons used in World War I, in the belief that an even greater world war is being predicted in Revelation 9.

When we look at the book he published on Revelation in 1908, we find similar language:

> Doesn't this fire and smoke and sulphur coming out of the mouths of the horses make us think of gunpowder and dynamite, as used in guns, cannons and machine guns, all three of which spew fire and smoke and sulphur out of their mouths with such explosive noise that it makes you shake? These weapons do not shrink back; they are horrible in their operation. Add the bombs and other explosives—"hellish weapons," as they are often called—that are used to cause death and destruction on a large scale. These things bring us closer to what John saw in his vision. Yet such modern weapons were still unknown to him. It was more than a millennium later—about 500 years ago—that gunpowder was invented, which in turn made guns, cannons, bombs, and other such weapons of war and instruments of destruction possible (p. 312).

Pay careful attention to what Greijdanus writes here: "These things bring us closer to what John saw in his vision. Yet such modern weapons were still unknown to him." From such statements it is clear that Greijdanus does in fact view the book of Revelation as some sort of "Handbook to the Future" speaking of events unknown to its authors, events that would first become clear through later developments. Otherwise he could not say that the invention of gunpowder and explosives brings this vision of John near for us, and that these things were still unknown to John himself.

This method of interpretation does not differ in principle from Hal Lindsey's method when it comes to such visions. For Lindsey the atom bomb is the key that opens up the meaning of such visions, while the emergence of Red China is also revealing:

> John describes the means by which one-third of mankind will be annihilated as "fire, smoke, and brimstone." All of these things are part of a thermonuclear war: smoke represents the immense clouds of radioactive fallout and debris, while brimstone is simply melted earth and building materials.
>
> Red China is not only a thermonuclear power at the time of this writing but the rapidity with which she became one is even more startling . . . .
>
> I personally believe that the "four evil angels" who will be unbound at the River Euphrates will instantly mobilize a giant war machine made up of some of the oriental countries, primarily Red China . . . (NW, 141-2).

As long as the book of Revelation is regarded as an oracle revealing secrets about future political and military developments, any well-intended orthodox exegesis in the style of Greijdanus will play right into the hands of the sectarians. They will then be seen only as carrying the interpretation a bit farther in a certain direction.

I remember my mother telling me about a certain preacher she knew who pointed to the invention of the automobile as the fulfillment of Nahum 2:4: "The chariots rage in the streets; they rush to and fro through the squares." We may laugh as we think of this old-fashioned preacher's consternation at the sight of the first horseless carriages, but his approach to Scripture cannot so easily be dismissed. Is the meaning of certain prophecies unveiled by modern inventions and developments—yes or no? If we say yes, the sectarian views of the dispensationalists are not so far off the mark.

Let's take another example. In Revelation 14:6 we read

about the angel with the "eternal" gospel who is bringing a
message to every nation. In his 1925 commentary,
Greijdanus writes: "How this is to come about is not indicated—apart from what we read in verse 7—but will
become apparent when the fulfillment comes." When he
wrote about the book of Revelation in the "Korte
Verklaring" series in 1938, he observed: "When we read
about the angel flying in midheaven, we think about the
radio, which enables us to make the gospel message heard
all over the world" (p. 227).

The radio had come into play between 1925 and 1938.
This technological advance brought with it an advance in
our understanding of the book of Revelation, according to
Greijdanus. These things were not yet clear to John!

As for the last verse of Revelation 17, which deals with
the "great city," it becomes an occasion for Greijdanus to
bring his political and cultural views about the future to expression. In his 1925 commentary, he writes:

> Here Rome appears in a certain capacity—as the capital city
> of a world empire. This shows us that we need not think
> exclusively in terms of Rome. What is meant is the world-
> city, the capital city of the world empire, which at that time
> was Rome but could later be some other city (p. 357).

It *could* be some other city. But from Greijdanus' interpretation of Revelation 17:10, it is apparent that it could
also remain Rome. "In the future it will be the great city of
the world empire of the Antichrist, whether that be Rome
or some other city" (p. 348). From here it is but a single step
to the claim made by Rev. I. de Wolff that Rome, the city
on the Tiber River, is indeed meant, and that in the future
Rome will be the city of the Antichrist (*De laatste Jaren der
Wereld*, published in 1960, p. 208). Futuristic speculation
reminiscent of Hal Lindsey!

In his book *De Antichrist*, Valentinus Hepp spoke of a
certain narrowing of consciousness after the Reformation.
(This book was published in 1919; the dates are important

in this discussion.) The Reformers, including Luther and Calvin, did not want to think in terms of a future antichrist; every pope was an antichrist. According to Hepp, this one-sidedness on their part is not to be approved or imitated. It can be compared with the conduct of a man who jumps out of the way of an automobile into the path of a moving streetcar (p. 136). After the Reformation, the belief that the Antichrist will be someone in the distant future was given up almost completely. In our time, Hepp goes on to say, people are returning to a much older position on this matter (p. 147).

Is Hepp's position really such an old one? Was it shared by the church fathers? I'm not so sure. But what concerns me especially is Hepp's appeal to go back behind the Reformation. Hepp shakes his head sadly as he explains that the Reformers saw antichrists among their contemporaries. Is he right to shake his head? And whose idea was it in the first place to go back behind the Reformation?

Hepp recognized that it was Pietism (J. A. Bengel, 1687-1752) that aroused fresh interest in the doctrine of the last things. He admits that the sectarians were especially concerned with this doctrine. Hepp writes: "With mysterious cords, the events of the day [1919] bind those who look to the Scriptures for light to the Bible's prophecy about the Antichrist" (p. 147). Hepp quotes Abraham Kuyper with approval when Kuyper writes that the book of Revelation does not present the history of the twentieth century but does tell us "what is still going to happen, what we await when the time of the end arrives." He then adds: "The truth we must hang on to is this, that if what John's Apocalypse, from chapter 7 on, tells us about has not taken place in the past or the present, then it is still to come and therefore awaits fulfillment" (p. 112).

Question: given this deliberate break with the Reformation, how far has Reformed exegesis and dogmatics managed to stay away from the apocalypticism of the Fundamentalists? The answer is: not very far. Dispensationalism—think of the Dallas Seminary statement—applies Revelation 6 and succeeding chapters to events that are still to come. Abraham Kuyper did the same thing, starting with chapter 7.

Hepp's great opponent was Klaas Schilder, who also chose for a futuristic interpretation of the prophetic passages in the New Testament. While Schilder never wrote about the "last things" in the context of formal dogmatics, it is clear from his publications that he did not differ essentially with Hepp on these matters but followed the futuristic line taken by Kuyper before him.

As we consider Schilder's position, we must remember that he, too, was a child of his time. His covenant emphasis was dynamite under the Fundamentalist eschatology, but Schilder never lit the fuse. He was dependent on the tradition in Reformed exegesis, and that tradition had not learned to be independent when dealing with the last things; it was not free from the influences that Hepp proposed to follow back behind the Reformation. Schilder was also subject to influences that were strong in his time, for he lived during the tense period between the two world wars. (Think of Hepp's references to the events of the day, and the wartime colors that sober Prof. Greijdanus introduced into his commentary on Revelation.) In this case, to know all is to forgive all.

This does not mean, however, that we can let the matter rest with a few such comments—especially now that Biblical apocalypticism is on the rise and finds so many useful points of contact within the Reformed tradition.

In his book *Operatie Supermens* (published in 1975), W. J. Ouweneel has written, from his Darbyistic standpoint:

> The most orthodox Christians, fortunately, are still convinced of the coming of a personal Antichrist . . . . The Antichrist spoken of in Scripture should not be thought of as a symbol for apostasy but as a flesh-and-blood renegade who will lead many astray . . . . All I wish to emphasize is what is already accepted among Bible-believing Christians, namely, that the end of our age will involve a worldwide occult idolatry in which the Antichrist takes the lead . . . .

Naturally, these predictions about the coming of the Antichrist will only speak to those who accept the Bible at its word. The remarkable thing is that there are so many symptoms that most people don't seem to notice, symptoms that clearly point to the end of our society (pp. 228-31).

Notice what is being presupposed here: (1) the acceptance of a personal Antichrist as a sign of orthodoxy, and (2) the dogma of a special "end time." We are also told that various phenomena in nature (e.g. earthquakes, hurricanes), in technology, and in culture are signs of the times, signs that the "end time" is near. The Bible's detail and accuracy in sketching the frightening signs of the times is awesome, we are told (p. 231).

The views of Ouweneel are an example of Fundamentalist apocalypticism. But the reason why such views catch on so quickly in Reformed circles is that we have virtually grown up with them. It all sounds vaguely familiar. Because we do not realize that this apocalypticism rises from a non-Reformed way of thinking, we utter no strong protest.

New Testament "apocalyptic" prophecy in the light of the covenant

The doctrine of the covenant is coming back into style. When scholars read the Old Testament, they are willing to take the covenant into account. But isn't the Old Testament somehow sub-Christian or pre-Christian? And doesn't the "new covenant" have an entirely different structure?

It's not so strange that in our world of solidarity, global thinking and universal social concern, the New Testament is read apart from the covenant. What we must realize is that dispensationalism operates within a similar framework in its reading of the New Testament, even though it does not share the liberal political and social ideals of those who preach solidarity and the social gospel.

Now, this loosing of the tie between the New Testament and the covenant has roots far in the past. Earlier I pointed to Marcion, the Anabaptists and Cocceius. Many Christians like to play off Christ against Moses, grace against the law. A classic example is the *Scofield Reference Bible's* treatment of John 1:17, a text that reads as follows:

A) For the law was given through Moses;
B) grace and truth came through Jesus Christ.

The *Scofield Bible* comments on this text as follows:

The point of testing is no longer legal obedience [i.e. obedience to the law given through Moses] as the condition of salvation, but acceptance or rejection of Christ, with good works as a fruit of salvation [i.e. "grace and truth"].

The old covenant under Moses is then portrayed as some sort of "covenant of works" and is contrasted with the "covenant of grace" established by Christ.

This interpretation of John 1:17, which is by no means foreign to the Reformed community, is based on false assumptions. Christ came to *fulfill* the law and the prophets—not to abolish them (Matt. 5:17). Moses already wrote about Christ (John 5:46). Neither Paul nor the Sermon on the Mount are opposed to the law as such (Gal. 3:10-12; Matt. 5:21-44), for the law is holy and righteous and good (I Tim. 1:8; Rom. 7:12,16). What Paul and Jesus opposed was the legalistic interpretation of the Judaism of their time, which militated against the law's original intention and purpose as doctrine and guidance from Yahweh.

The law of Moses was the law of Yahweh, the God of the covenant. For that reason alone, it may not be contrasted with the grace and truth brought by Christ, the Son of the Father (John 1:14, 18). The "truth" referred to in part B of John 1:17 does not stand over against untruth or falsity in part A. "Truth" is a typological term referring to realization, fulfillment. Part A refers to the model, the shadow, the prefiguration of the law in Moses, while part B speaks of the fulfillment, the truth (*veritas*). Part A is the typological prefiguration, while part B is the realization of the model.

The kind of language we encounter here was already used by Melito of Sardis in an Easter sermon preached around the year 170:

A) The example is temporary;
B) grace is eternal.
A) The prefiguration was present;
B) the truth has been found.

We also find such language in Article 25 of the Belgic Confession of Faith, which opposes the views of the Anabaptists, who took a dim view of the Israelites and the Old Testament. We read:

> We believe that the symbols and ceremonies of the law ceased at the coming of Christ, and that all the shadows are accomplished; so that the use of them must be abolished among Christians; yet the truth (*veritas*) and substance (*substantia*) of them remain with us in Jesus Christ, in whom they have their completion.

It is essential for us to grasp the connection between parts A and B of John 1:17 in the proper light, for the point at issue is fundamental to the understanding and interpretation of the New Testament. In other words, what we must learn to do is read the New Testament in the light of God's covenant with His people.

In Reformed circles we claim to adhere to the doctrine that God's covenant is *one*. But have we worked enough with the implications of this doctrine? If so, why are so many of our people taken in by dispensationalist thinking?

After World War II, the Americans were the only ones who possessed the atom bomb. But it was precisely in this period that they lost so much influence—Russia, China, East Germany, and so forth. They did not know how to exploit their advantage; they had no strategy to go with their power. The Reformed people are making the same mistake with their doctrine of the covenant. They don't know how to make maximum use of that doctrine when it comes to interpreting the prophetic, "apocalyptic" passages in the New Testament.

They fail to deal with passages like Matthew 24, II Thessalonians 2, and Revelation 6-18 as covenant prophecy addressed to God's covenant people, as prophecy that deals with their future against the background of the covenant relationship. Instead they rip these passages from their covenant context and apply them to some strange, bizarre, faraway "end time." Thereby they read the New Testament by different rules than the Old Testament.

When John spoke of "grace and truth," no one wanted to argue that he was referring to a distant "end time." Everyone agreed: the prophecies of grace found their realization in Jesus Christ. "Today this Scripture has been fulfilled in your hearing" (Luke 4:21). Then why not be consistent and apply the covenant threats of the Old Testament, which are repeated in the New Testament, to the present as well—instead of to some vague future age? Christ came to bring about the realization of grace and judgment—starting in His own era on earth! In that way He fulfilled the "law." Using the structure of John 1:17, we could say:

A) The law with its sanctions (threats) was given by Moses;
B) truth (the fulfillment of those sanctions) and judgment came through Jesus Christ.

All I have done with John 1:17 is to replace "grace" with "judgment." Read through the gospels and see how often Christ says that He came for purposes of judgment. Even though He is referring in part to the final judgment, He also intends to set a few things straight before then. Whoever rejects the "today of grace" will be subject to the "today of judgment." When Christ talks about outbursts of judgment, He is not just referring to catastrophes in the distant future, just as His talk of grace is not meant for the distant future alone. The prophetic element in His style of address brings out the contemporary covenant relevance of His words, all the way through the book of Revelation.

In his book *Zijn ene Woord* (1974), Rev. G. Van Rongen has made some comments worthy of careful attention. He points out that the Bible speaks of many days of the Lord or days of Yahweh, which are days of covenant judgment. In this regard the New Testament is no different from the Old. Doesn't the book of Revelation talk repeatedly about an early coming of Christ? (see 2:5, 25). Such language should be taken seriously, Van Rongen argues. The destruction of Jerusalem in the year 70 must be seen as a surprising coming of Christ on His day of covenant judgment (pp. 30-76).

When we read the New Testament in its covenant context, we see that Israel is placed before a momentous choice—either repent and accept Christ as the promised Messiah or be destroyed. That choice cannot be taken lightly.

In his Pentecost sermon, Peter speaks clear language (Acts 2:14ff). Blood and fire and vapors of smoke were coming in the "last days"—and they did come not much later, in the year 70, when Jerusalem was destroyed. This frightening event should serve as a sign to the later church that it may perish too if it is unfaithful.

Futuristic projection of prophecies into a distant "end time" has had the effect of masking the covenantal character and framework of such passages. And this, in turn, has left the dispensationalists plenty of room to build their eschatological system.

In this context I must point to the great uncertainty even in Reformed circles about the question of the "future of Israel." In his lengthy commentary on Romans, for example, Greijdanus speaks openly of the impending conversion of Israel (p. 516). When he deals with Luke 13:35 in his lengthy commentary on Luke, he speaks similar language. This text refers to Israel's conversion, he assures us. "A plural form is used here—Jerusalem, the Jewish people as a whole." This great conversion will occur around the time of the Lord's return (Vol. II, p. 683).

Here Greijdanus deliberately chooses to oppose Calvin and take the side of post-Reformation Pietism: Israel awaits a restoration. For various reasons, such views linger in the Reformed community to this day. No one seems to know quite what to make of the survival of the Jews as an identifiable ethnic group and the rise of the state of Israel. This leaves the door open to the acceptance of sectarian views.

As long as the covenant is not taken seriously as a prerogative and privilege of the New Testament church, the uncertainty will persist. The New Testament clearly refers to the Jews as the covenant people of that time, as we saw earlier. But the same New Testament also threatens the Jews with covenant wrath if they reject the Messiah. That covenant wrath struck in the year 70. After that it no longer made sense to say that the Jews enjoyed covenant privileges as a special people.

It sounds simple, but what are interpreters in our time doing? That "last word" of covenant judgment is ignored, and people still "await" something with regard to Israel. On the other hand, when the New Testament speaks of judgment on an apostate covenant people in Matthew 24, II Thessalonians 2 and the book of Revelation (warnings that are meant as a sign for us as well), they want to hear nothing of an interpretation in covenantal terms. These passages are read as talking about general judgments and future calamities in the world.

What these prophecies are alleged to give us, then, is an outline of the eschatological future, a blueprint that includes some of the details. That way the prophecies are cut adrift from their moorings to bob on the sea of world history so that we can be assured of that gruesome, frightening "end time" we so often see just around the corner. We insist on an eschatological program of events that are yet to come.

We must rethink our approach to eschatology, using

God's covenant with His people as our starting point. While Matthew 24, II Thessalonians 2 and the book of Revelation have a great deal to say to us, we must learn to recognize them as prophecies of covenant wrath that have been fulfilled in the judgment that struck Israel and stripped her of her covenant privileges. The God of the covenant remains one and the same, and He does not alter the structure of His covenant.

As we rethink our approach to eschatology, we will have to surrender beloved interpretations of certain texts. Not everything served up as sound exegesis should be accepted as such.

We must also bear in mind that exegetical literature written in English or German rarely reckons with the covenant, for the covenant does not play a major role in Methodist or Pietist thinking. Exegesis is never neutral; the exegete's own confession plays a role in shaping his results. Therefore, if exegetes pay little attention to the covenant in their own thinking, we need not expect them to make much of the covenant as an exegetical key. As for liberal and Modernistic interpreters, they don't have much to say about the covenant either. Human solidarity and philosophizing about man in general is more important to them than the covenant as the framework for interpreting both the Old Testament and the New.

Therefore we must look critically at widely accepted interpretations of the Bible and learn to stand on our own feet. We, too, live by the Bible in our covenant relationship with our Lord. If we sense the power of that covenant relationship in our own lives, let's not be afraid to demand a recognition of the covenant as we read and evaluate Fundamentalist interpretations of Scripture. The Fundamentalists ignore the covenant and oversimplify many matters in a mad scramble to put together an exciting dispensationalist eschatological calendar.

All around us we see people ignoring or openly denying the covenantal character of our relationship to our God. This process has gone much farther than many of us suspect. Even in seemingly conservative circles, the covenant is often ignored in Biblical interpretation.

Some of the newer Bible translations have helped this process along—especially the so-called "modern" ones. These translations tend to let go of covenant language in their eagerness to reach modern man, who no longer knows what marriage or other such covenants are about and insists on a brief, easy-to-grasp presentation of the gospel. In their determination to present the Bible's message in twentieth century language clear to secular man and the most naive, childlike Christians, these translations throw caution to the winds and don't worry about precision. After all, they have to compete against the paraphrased versions of the Bible!

The result of this process is that the Bible message becomes more and more unclear and subjective. Old Testament texts and concepts are hardly recognizable in the text of the New Testament, where they are echoed. The unity of the covenant language spoken by the Lord is lost. The result is a new generation of Christians who no longer hear the voice of the God of the covenant speaking to them in the New Testament.

Therefore there is work to be done. We must fight for a covenantal understanding of the Bible—Old Testament and New. An emphasis on the unity of the covenant will enable us to defend ourselves against the propaganda about the "church age" and the special "end time."

There is work to be done especially on the book of Revelation. When it comes time to assess the dispensationalist interpretation of Revelation found in Hal Lindsey's writings, the orthodox pot is hardly in a position to reproach the Darbyist kettle, for the two share the same thought structure to a surprising degree.

It is not enough to point out Hal Lindsey's errors. If Lindsey is wrong in his reading of the book of Revelation, what interpretation are we to put in its place?

A Prophecy of Covenant Wrath for Jerusalem

Generally agreed?

It has been shown that Revelation 16-19 cannot be applied to the destruction of Jerusalem without doing violence to the text. This is what F. Lücke argued back in 1852 in his book *Einleitung in die Offenbarung des Johannes*. It is generally agreed, he reported, that these chapters in the book of Revelation deal with the destruction of the heathen city of Rome. In the strict historical sense, this prophecy was never fulfilled, Lücke admits (pp. 836-8, 855, 861). But this does not undermine the Bible's credibility, he goes on to say, for the image or outward wrapper must be distinguished from the idea within. Thus Lücke makes use of a form/content distinction and proposes to demythologize the book of Revelation. The heart of the book is what it says about the Antichrist, of whom Nero's Rome is only a type. Thus Lücke has a cork to plug each hole in his theory.

That was the nineteenth century. What about our time? What is "generally agreed" today? A. J. Visser, in his book *De Openbaring van Johannes* (1965), argues that John awaited a return of the Roman emperor Nero that never took place (pp. 130, 233-4). But the issue, again, is the *kernel* of the message. "When it comes to understanding the real message of John's Apocalypse, it is not a matter of life and death to find out on historical grounds whether the author was frustrated in his expectation." John was preparing his readers for a struggle that would rage throughout the ages. "What he saw in the brightest colors in his vision never actually took place in the form in which he expected it, but similar struggles have indeed taken place repeatedly and could come again at any moment."

The Jerusalem Bible (1966) identifies Babylon with Rome, as does the *New Bible Commentary* (1970). In its treatment of Revelation 17 (by G. R. Beasley-Murray), it breathes new life into the idea that a resurrected Nero is meant.

Contemporary political events, the development of the secular city, the astounding technological advances of our time—all of this has contributed toward the survival of mistaken interpretations of the book of Revelation developed in earlier centuries. One of the few exceptions is a book of 1939 by V. Burch entitled *Anthropology and the Apocalypse*, in which Revelation is examined in the light of Jewish symbols. But this exception confirms the rule: there is no place for the view that the "Babylon" referred to in Revelation is Jerusalem rather than Rome and no place for a covenantal interpretation. This, indeed, is "generally agreed"—in conservative and liberal circles alike.

Benne Holwerda

Writing contemporary history is not easy. Writing contemporary church history is still harder. Thus, dealing with the history of the interpretation of the book of Revelation in our time poses various perils. Still, I cannot pass over the contribution made by Prof. Benne Holwerda (1909-52) without comment, for Holwerda unleashed more than he realized in 1949. On various occasions he delivered a certain address and finally published it under the title *De Kerk in het Eindgericht* (The Church in the Final Judgment). He then went on to defend his viewpoint in a periodical entitled *De Reformatie*.

Holwerda can hardly be branded an adherent of the view that the Babylon mentioned in the book of Revelation is

Jerusalem. He accepts it as generally agreed that the sixth head of the beast represents the Roman empire and that the seven hills are a reference to Rome, the city built on seven hills. Holwerda divides the visions into two series: chapters 4-11, which focus on the *world*, and chapters 12-22, which focus on the *church*.

Holwerda's interpretation of Revelation 17 was hardly new. In fact, it had been in circulation for a long time and even found some support in the notes attached to the Dutch counterpart of the King James Bible. Yet, defending that interpretation in 1949 caused some excitement, because of conditions in the Dutch churches at the time.

Holwerda's position was that the woman in Revelation 17 is *not* the Roman empire with all its cultural treasures. "Babylon" and the woman were the "false church." He presented the following arguments in favor of his interpretaton.

(1) It is apparent from Revelation 2:9 that John knows of a community that claims to be a congregation of the living God but is really a synagogue of satan.

(2) Revelation 17 clearly echoes Exodus 16 and 23, where Israel is branded a harlot who fails to keep the covenant.

(3) The great city is also mentioned in Revelation 11:8, where a political-cultural interpretation is out of the question. This suggests that Babylon should not be identified as a political-cultural entity in Revelation 17 and 18 either.

(4) It is made clear in the book of Acts (see 2:23; 3:13; 4:10; 5:30; 7:52) that it was Jerusalem that opposed Jesus, although Rome did in fact carry out the death sentence. Jesus was crucified in the great city that is Spiritually called Sodom and Egypt.

(5) It is apparent from Revelation 18:20 that when the harlot is destroyed, God is squaring accounts because of what she has done to the prophets and apostles. Four verses later we read: "In her was found the blood of prophets and of saints." This includes the Old Testament believers who died in Jerusalem. Even under the old covenant, "the

woman" played a role as the murderer of God's servants and children. "The people of Israel have slain thy prophets" (I Kings 19:10). Jesus speaks of "the righteous blood shed on earth" (Matt. 23:35).

(6) Revelation 18:22-3 echoes Jeremiah 25:10, which deals with Jerusalem explicitly.

Although Holwerda operated within a certain traditional framework, he presented an interpretation that differed from the usual view as defended by Greijdanus, for example. No wonder that he was criticized from various sides. C. P. Plooy argued that Holwerda's exegesis was a foolish mistake: throughout the book of Revelation, the great city is Rome of those days as a type of the great world-city at the end of time.

Herman Ridderbos, the well-known New Testament scholar, responded to Holwerda, pointing out that Greijdanus stayed away from any identification of the great harlot of Revelation 17-18 with the false church. (Greijdanus was not the only one, of course.) Ridderbos added that he knew of no reputable exegete who even took this possibility seriously. The great harlot of Revelation 17 is not the church but the world, he declared.

Familiar sounds indeed. "Most interpreters today" were cited as an argument against Holwerda. Frequent appeals were made to Greijdanus. The debate began to take on an emotional flavor; strong language was used.

Holwerda himself did not respond to Ridderbos, but Klaas Schilder, one of his colleagues, did. Although Schilder himself had always followed Greijdanus on the interpretation of the book of Revelation, he came to the defense of his colleague Holwerda. He pointed out that R. H. Charles, a scholar with a distinguished reputation, argued that the writer of Revelation 17:16 must have had the text of Exodus 23:25-9 before him. Ezekiel 23 deals with the harlotry of "Oholibah," which makes us think of the false church and unfaithfulness to the covenant. What we read about Jerusalem in the book of Revelation is reminiscent of this passage in Ezekiel, Schilder pointed out (see *De Reformatie*, XXV, 1949-50, p. 287).

In his debate with Ridderbos, Schilder also pointed out that Charles speaks of early *Jewish* sources in connection with Revelation 13, 17 and 18, sources that the alleged editor of Revelation then reworked (see *Revelation*, I, pp. lxii-lxv, 334-8; II, pp. 88-9, 94-5, 59-60). Hence the Jewish flavor to the description of the burning of the harlot. According to Leviticus 21:9, a priest's daughter who became a harlot was to be burned to death (see *De Reformatie*, May 27, July 11 and August 12, 1950).

The important thing here is that Holwerda—and even Schilder, to some extent—recognizes the language of the book of revelation as *covenantal*. This recognition creates a new possibility, namely, that the opposition in Revelation is not between the church and the world. There is another opposition to be considered—the conflict between the church and the synagogue of satan.

That such a possibility was not instantly accepted in the climate that led to the formation of the World Council of Churches is understandable. Still, the direction suggested by Holwerda and Schilder should have been explored.

Twenty-five years later

In the 1930s, there was a renewed appreciation for the Scriptures in the Reformed churches of the Netherlands. The centrality of the covenant was recognized, as was redemptive history. It was realized that the Bible is not a source book containing moral examples and models for Christian living.

The positive effects of this renewed understanding and appreciation of Scripture were felt beyond World War II and into the 1950s. Think of such names as S. G. De Graaf, M. B. van't Veer, Klaas Schilder, and Benne Holwerda. But what happened after that? Where do we stand today, 25 years later?

One would expect that the study of Scripture from a

redemptive historical standpoint would be continued vigorously. There was a great deal of work to be done with the Old Testament as well as the New. In the case of the Old Testament, it had become clear that covenant wrath played a major role in the preaching of the prophets. It was recognized that the Psalms could not be interpreted properly on the basis of the opposition between the church and the world. The background to the complaints uttered by the psalmists was the struggle with false brothers—not foreign enemies.

What about the New Testament? Isn't it full of the antithesis between the church and the world? Or were the writers of the New Testament constantly trying to draw a line between the church and the synagogue of satan? Was a chapter like Matthew 24 talking about judgment in general or covenant wrath? And what about the book of Revelation? Was it really written in opposition to the beast in Rome? If so, it would be out of step with the rest of the New Testament and the attitudes of the earliest Christian writers.

There were many more such questions to be asked. And they should have been answered on the basis of the newly won insight into the unity of the Scriptures and the covenant. Much of the study material in use would have to be rewritten since it was based on a non-covenantal view of Scripture and a mistaken understanding of the covenant.

Also significant is that there were all sorts of foreign influences that had left their mark on the widely accepted interpretation of Scripture. Those influences could have been combatted on the basis of the new view of the Scriptures—and especially the New Testament—developed in the 1930s.

That's what *should* have happened—but it didn't. As Sidney Greijdanus has pointed out, the interest in redemptive historical preaching declined sharply (see his dissertation, *Sola Scriptura*, published in English in 1970). Rev. Gilbert VanDooren admitted in 1975 that the struggle for redemptive historical preaching has not progressed very far, and that this approach has not yet been properly applied to the study of the New Testament (*Clarion*, XXIV, Sept. 19, 1975). Even in churches seemingly committed to a redemptive historical reading of the Bible, elements of Chiliasm are still to be found. VanDooren mentions a preacher who is convinced that the church will one day be "transported" to Jerusalem, where the Jews will be ready for King Jesus. The Christians and Jews will live together in a kingdom of Christ until the end of time, when there will be a short but horrible period in which satan is allowed to run loose. VanDooren mentions another preacher who keeps insisting that the time is near for a mass conversion of the Jews to Christianity. He points to a leading figure who is convinced that the Reformed confessions must make room for the "truth" that the Jews are still God's covenant people in a special sense.

The examples cited by VanDooren show that there has been little—if any—progress in Reformed circles in deepening the covenantal, redemptive historical approach to the Scriptures. Why? One reason is the untimely death of both Schilder and Holwerda in 1952. Another reason is the ecclesiastical struggle of the time—although that is by no means an excuse. (Ecclesiastical warfare didn't hold Calvin and Luther back from the task of reformation!) A third reason is that not enough attention was paid to the good work already done.

Now, I don't mean to deny that there were elements of Fundamentalism in the thinking of Schilder and Holwerda, strange doctrines that were untenable when held up to the bright light of Scripture. Think of their expectation of a special "end time," a period to be dominated by a cultural-political human monster—the Antichrist. Think also of their exegesis of Revelation, which was based on faulty assumptions.

Yet Holwerda should not be judged too harshly. He was called away in the middle of his work. Thus there was little time for him to raise the question whether the covenant context he had supplied for the interpretation of Revelation

17 might have further consequences for the interpretation of Revelation as a whole. It is noteworthy that Schilder was willing to listen to him on this point. But this should not strike us as strange, for Schilder, like Holwerda, stressed the centrality of the covenant.

What is so unfortunate is that the direction taken by Holwerda in connection with Revelation 17 was not pursued farther. Instead more and more elements of Fundamentalism were drawn into the discussion about the book of Revelation. The beloved themes of the "end time" and the "Antichrist" kept rising to the surface.

We see this reflected, for example, in *Nederlands Dagblad*, a Reformed daily newspaper in the Netherlands. Consider the following quotations, which are taken from editorials published in 1968 and 1969:

> These developments are indeed frightening. The contours of a world of the end time, such as the book of Revelation sketches, are becoming clearer and clearer. In that world the faithful church will have an even harder time of it. [Then comes the usual quotation from Matthew 24:32-3: "From the fig tree learn its lesson . . . . So also, when you see all these things, you know that he is near, at the very gates."]
>
> We are systematically being driven in the direction of a "brave new world" in which the ten commandments will be replaced by some new rules of the game that the brain trust of a new world government will establish.
>
> It may well be that the plan will succeed. In fact, God's Word predicts that man will create such a world at the end of time. That world will not be Paradise Regained but the great city of Babylon, not the new earth to which God's children look forward eagerly but the horrible world of the Antichrist.

Here we find all the typical elements—a steady evolution of evil, the presence of "signs of the times," an application of the fig tree lesson in the style of Hal Lindsey to contemporary events, the view that God's Word characterizes a certain period at the end of history as the "end time," and the expectation of an antichrist as a world dictator.

Orwell and Huxley have made such an impression that "Babylon" is now interpreted in cultural-political terms rather than covenantal terms. "Babylon" is identified with the cities presented in contemporary pipe dreams about the future. Visions of the Antichrist are applied to the society of the future and the city of the future as sketched by Hendrik Van Riessen and Egbert Schuurman. But the line that Holwerda began to draw, the line that proceeds from the centrality of the covenant and the church in the book of Revelation—that line was not continued.

Holwerda's work was only a beginning. Because of his untimely death, it remained a torso. His views about the book of Revelation were still too much mired in the old political interpretation that starts with Rome. But he did bring the covenant to bear on this book. The harlot of Revelation 17 was understood in relation to *the church*!

Holwerda achieved a certain popularity in Reformed circles. His ideas were widely discussed. But that was more than 25 years ago. And even then his thinking was placed in the wrong exegetical framework. The most valuable element in his thought—the covenantal approach to such prophecies as Revelation 17—gradually disappeared from sight. In the circles of his supposed admirers one could hear such comments as the following:

> The book of Revelation makes no reference whatsoever to the earthly, Palestinian Jerusalem. "Jerusalem" is mentioned only at the end, when John talks about the city of the future, the eschatological city.

> It can be accepted as established that the last book of the Bible was not given to us as an apocalyptic account of judgments that were carried out centuries ago on the former city of God, the Palestinian Jerusalem. Anyone who preaches on a text from Revelation must not act as though the prophecies of that book were fulfilled in the destruction of Jerusalem.

Compare these comments with what Holwerda himself had to say:

All these passages in Acts [2:23; 3:13; 4:10; 5:30; 7:52] strengthen me in my conviction that the "great city" in Revelation is *Jerusalem,* the city of the *church.* This does not mean that every reference to the "great city" must be read exclusively as a reference to "Jerusalem." But I would come close to saying that, especially on the basis of Revelation 16:19, where the "great city" is distinguished from "the cities of the *nations.*" To me this suggests that the "great city" is one and the same throughout the book of Revelation (including 17:18), and that we are to think of it as the false church.

Despite his inclinations toward a futuristic interpretation of Revelation, then, Holwerda points clearly in the direction of a covenantal interpretation that makes the church central.

Holwerda made himself sufficiently clear, but even his supposed followers are hesitant about going along with him here. Why? Why is Holwerda's appeal to the Old Testament as basic to understanding the book of Revelation ignored? Why is the traditional interpretation so hard to shake?

We are not facing a mere academic question here. Could it be that the generally accepted exegesis is supported by a certain perspective on Scripture, a perspective that implicitly dismisses the Old Testament as "Jewish," as one possible realization of a universal religious ideal? Isn't this in fact the dominant approach to Scripture nowadays?

If we accept this approach, it is natural to conclude that the book of Revelation, whose language echoes the threats of covenant wrath in Leviticus 26, points not to covenant judgment but to a catastrophe that will strike a world-city someday. In the process we turn the last book in the Bible into an apocalyptic tract that belongs on the library shelf next to Orwell and Huxley. The book of Revelation then becomes science fiction—precisely because we first assumed that it is mere speculation to argue that it points to the same kind of covenant judgment that Jesus announced in Matthew 24.

This approach plays into the hands of both Modernism and Fundamentalism. The Modernist is the great leveler; he wants to universalize everything and put everyone on the same level. That's why he embraces modernized Bible translations with their misleading headings. Any traces of the covenant left in that modernized Bible he will erase in his preaching, meditation and exegesis. After all, the Bible is meant for man in general—not for God's covenant people alone!

As for Fundamentalism in its current dispensationalist garb, it isn't eager to talk about the covenant either. After all, the old covenant has an entirely different structure than the new covenant! What the book of Revelation tells us in language reminiscent of the Old Testament must be translated into twentieth century language; its message must be explained in terms of general truths about a horrible "end time" to come. Fundamentalism turns the book of Revelation into a forerunner of Velikovsky's *Worlds in Collision.*

What a shame that the work begun by Holwerda was never carried further! There was plenty of reason to take up the suggestions he threw out for consideration, but it appears that his comments have been forgotten. The stone he threw into the exegetical pond caused some ripples around 1950, but now the pond's surface is once more as smooth as a sheet of ice.

Two noteworthy publications

John A. T. Robinson is well known for his controversial book *Honest to God.* What the general public does not know is that he is a New Testament scholar who has made some beautiful observations about the background to the Gospel according to John. Robinson points to the clash between the church and the "synagogue."

In 1976 he published a book that will surely cause raised eyebrows among New Testament scholars—*Re-*

dating the New Testament. In this book he pleads for a redating of the entire New Testament, including the book of Revelation. He argues that not one of the New Testament books reports the destruction of Jerusalem as an accomplished fact. This is not so strange, for the entire New Testament was written before the year 70!

I agree with this conclusion wholeheartedly, although I do not agree with all the arguments Robinson uses to support it. (For my views on the dating of the various New Testament books, see the four New Testament volumes of *Search the Scriptures*, also published by Paideia Press.) I am convinced that New Testament scholarship must take the direction that Robinson has indicated. Isn't it ironic that a man like Robinson, who is not noted for his commitment to orthodoxy, pleads for an earlier dating of the New Testament and thereby opens the door to a renewed understanding of the Bible as a whole?

Robinson's breakthrough is just that—a breakthrough. There is still a great deal that remains to be done. Robinson himself reads the book of Revelation as referring to Rome when it speaks of "Babylon."

There is another noteworthy publication to which we should give our attention, by someone not as well known as Robinson. This publication points in the direction of the view that Babylon is Jerusalem.

In 1975, the year of the woman, a commentary on the book of Revelation was published in the "Anchor Bible" series, which is an international project involving birds of diverse plumage—Protestants, Catholics, Jews. That commentary has some surprising things to say. The author of the commentary is Josephine M. Ford, a remarkable woman who studied in London, taught in Uganda, and is now connected with Notre Dame, a Roman Catholic university in South Bend, Indiana. She is associated with those who plead for openness to the charismatic movement within the Roman Catholic Church. She is the author of various theological publications, some of which testify to considerable daring, originality, and almost naiveté.

Her discussion of the book of Revelation is hardly a run-of-the-mill treatment. She proposes the dubious thesis that chapters 4-11 stem from a circle of disciples of John the Baptist and reflect his *initial* expectations of the one who was to come, that is, *before* he found out about the life and work of Christ. Chapters 12-22 come from a different circle of disciples of John the Baptist, disciples who knew and accepted the teachings of Christ as well. They talked about the fall of Jerusalem because of their opposition to the Jews who rejected Christ. As for chapters 1-3 and certain other verses (i.e. 22:16a, 20b, 21), they were added by Jewish Christians with a still better knowledge of Christ, the kind of knowledge that Apollos used in his work in Ephesus (see Acts 18:24-8).

This most eccentric hypothesis can hardly be accepted as gospel truth. On the other hand, there is no denying that Ford has made a point that deserves careful attention, namely, that the book of Revelation should be read against the background of the work of John the Baptist and the antithesis within the Jewish covenant people.

Ford works out her viewpoint and comes to the conclusion that the judgment announced in the book of Revelation is *covenant wrath*. She points to the close connections between Leviticus 26 (the threat of sevenfold judgment) and the sevenfold plague in Revelation. According to her, Revelation 17 is influenced most of all by Exodus 16, "which is a prophetical attack on Jerusalem" (p. 283). She also identifies other texts dealing with the covenant as part of the background to Revelation 17 (Hos. 2:4; 3:3; 4:15; Is. 1:4, 9, 21; Jer. 2:20; Ezek. 23).

Ford likewise points to a prophecy against Jerusalem in a non-canonical Qumran scroll. (In the Qumran literature, much is made of the antithesis within the Jewish people.) What all these texts indicate is that the harlot of Revelation 17 is Jerusalem—not Rome. As long as covenant communion with Yahweh makes Israel His special people, His bride, how can a non-Israelite nation be reproached for harlotry and unfaithfulness? "It is the covenant which makes the bride," Ford argues. Only because there is a covenant can the bride be guilty of adultery (p. 285).

In 17:18, as well as 11:18 and 16:19, the "great city" referred to is Jerusalem (pp. 180, 292). It is significant that the "great city" is burned in judgment, for burning is the punishment reserved for a priest's daughter who plays the harlot (see Lev. 21:9).

Ford does not restrict herself to Qumran sources. She also points to Jewish motifs on a mosaic floor. The book of Revelation talks about the lampstand, the ram's horn, the lamb—typical Jewish symbols, as she emphasizes.

Did Ford come up with these ideas on her own, or was she picking up suggestions made by other scholars? Her bibliography does not mention Holwerda or Schilder or the early German scholars who made such suggestions (i.e. F. Abauzit, J. J. Wettstein, J. C. Harenberg, F. G. Hartwig). Apparently this scholar in the field of "religious studies" discovered these connections through her own research.

In 1974 Heinrich Kraft published a commentary on Revelation in the "Handbuch zum Neuen Testament" series. His book deserves attention because he recognizes that the city that opposes God and kills the prophets (11:8) is *Jerusalem*. However, when Kraft deals with Revelation 17, he forgets this insight and starts talking about Rome in the usual fashion. As for Revelation 18, it deals with some sort of abstract world-city of commerce, a concept already captured in Augustine's earthly city (civitas terrena).

Kraft turns Revelation into an exceedingly complex book, a veritable hodge-podge of ideas and symbols. Is this the best that contemporary exegesis can do? For one and the same motif (the "great city"), three entirely different meanings are suggested. No wonder the Germans talk about being "perplexed by apocalypticism" (*Ratlos vor der Apokalyptik*—the title of a recent book by Klaus Koch). German exegesis of Revelation seems to have reached a dead end.

That's all the more reason to be thankful for J. M. Ford's

suggestion that we read Revelation against the background
of the Old Testament and other Judaic writings. More than
25 years ago, Herman Ridderbos dismissed an attempt to
read Revelation 17 in covenantal terms by declaring that he
knew of no reputable exegete who even took this possibility
seriously. But now, from an unexpected direction, a new
scholarly commentary arrives on the scene and emphasizes
the covenant: "It is the covenant which makes the bride."
Doesn't this give us something to think about?

Fortunately, the study of the history of exegesis is not
always a dry business. Now and then we come across
something that makes us chuckle or smile. Thus there has
been some progress after all in these past 25 years—but not
where we expected.

Melito's Easter homily

In 1940 an ancient Easter homily was published in London and Philadelphia: *The Homily on the Passion by
Melito Bishop of Sardis.* This book gives the text of a papyrus
document drawn in part from the Chester Beatty Collection
and in part from the University of Michigan's holdings.
The papyrus had been found in Egypt in the 1930s.

The content of the papyrus was a sermon preached in the
passion season by Melito of Sardis. The existence of this
sermon was long known through the writings of Eusebius,
but no copy was located until the twentieth century. A subsequent papyrus find yielded a second copy of this sermon,
which was published in 1960.

Now, 1940 was not a particularly good year to arouse interest in an Easter homily. Everyone was preoccupied with
the question whether Hitler would invade England. Once
the war was over, the discovery of the Dead Sea Scrolls was
the most important piece of news. As a result, it was not
generally realized that Melito's Easter homily could make a
great contribution to the understanding of the book of
Revelation.

This homily is a sermon delivered by a pastor in one of the congregations mentioned in the book of Revelation— Sardis. It was delivered around the year 170, which is roughly when Sagar died as a martyr in Laodicea. In Revelation 3:1-3, Sardis is reproached by the Lord: it was rumored to be alive, but it was really dead. We must not interpret this text in deterministic fashion, as if to say, "Once a thief, always a thief!" The Word of the Lord had apparently struck home: Sardis came back to life and returned to the confession. This the sermon of Melito makes clear. The fact that Sagar became a martyr in Laodicea indicates that a similar revival took place there.

How can we be sure that Sardis had revived? This question is important for the exegesis of Revelation. The answer is surprising because of the light it sheds on our basic question about the book of Revelation, namely, whether Revelation sheds tears about Jerusalem or about Rome.

Sardis had awakened to the point of taking a clear stand over against the "synagogue of satan," just as Smyrna and Philadelphia had done earlier. In his sermon Melito explains clearly that Jesus Christ has fulfilled the shadows and models of the old covenant.

In those days it was customary in Asia Minor for the Christians to celebrate Easter at the same time that the Jews celebrated the Passover—the fourteenth day of the month Nisan. Those who advocated this practice came to be known as the Quartodecimans. This custom may go all the way back to the ancient church in Jerusalem. Polycrates of Ephesus reported around 190 that the apostle John decreed that this custom was to be maintained.

The conflict between the Christians and the Jews tended to flare up especially during the Passover season. Acts 12 reports that it was in this season that James was executed and Peter was put in prison. Polycarp, who was also in favor of the Quartodeciman custom and was even willing to undertake a journey to the bishop of Rome to promote it, may well have been put to death at a Passover feast (a "great sabbath"). Earlier we saw that Sagar died a martyr's death in Laodicea during the Passover season, with the Jews no doubt responsible.

It bothered the Jews intensely that the Christians refused to join in their feasts but prayed for their conversion instead. The beginning of the Gospel according to John must also be read in this light: it speaks about the Lamb of God and mentions the Passover feast three times. Paul emphasizes that Christ has been sacrificed as *"our paschal lamb"* (I Cor. 5:7). Peter likewise speaks of Jesus Christ as the Lamb (I Pet. 1:19). And Revelation, of course, must be read against the background of such language.

Melito's homily *Peri Pascha* (PP) confirms this. Opposition to the Jews is expressed throughout, and it ends with a stinging indictment. Also noteworthy is the fact that this sermon is based on Exodus 12—which was not unusual for early Christian Easter sermons—and makes *the Lamb* central (the Lamb that struck Egypt), just as the book of Revelation does. Given the text Melito chose, this should not surprise us. Yet this tradition and this choice of a text embody and reflect an intention, a certain concern related to the message of the book of Revelation. After all, the bishop of *Sardis* would be keenly interested in the book of Revelation!

Melito's homily is another indication that we are on the right track in making opposition to the Jews—rather than opposition to Rome—the central theme in the book of Revelation. To Melito, the Lord's covenant judgment on Jerusalem is part of history.

Just as the slaughtered Lamb defeated Egypt at the time of the Exodus (PP, 60), so Israel has been punished for the murder of the Lord. The temple is already destroyed; it lies there dead. Melito does not opt for a futuristic interpretation of Matthew 24, as Irenaeus does.

Peri Pascha sheds some significant light on Revelation 11:8, where we read about the bodies of the two witnesses lying in the *plateia* (the street, the square) of the great city that is Spiritually called Sodom and *Egypt*. As we have already seen, some interpreters are willing to concede that this reference to the "great city" points to Jerusalem, but others deny it. Many sense that it would be strange if Revelation meant Jerusalem on one occasion when it spoke of the "great city" and Rome on another occasion. The obvious assumption is that the term has the same meaning in both occurrences.

In Greijdanus's 1938 commentary on Revelation (in the "Korte Verklaring" series), Revelation 11 refers to events that have yet to take place. Such an interpretation, however, might encourage people to hope for a rebuilding of the temple. To combat that misconception, Greijdanus emphasized that Revelation 11 was not about future events in the *Palestinian* Jerusalem. He wanted to do all he could to head off any adventist or Chiliast interpretation. Hence his next step. Jerusalem is referred to here only "insofar as it is a type—just as Sodom and Egypt are types—of the great city and anti-Christian power in its misdeeds against the Lord's gospel, service and believers" (p. 182). Because of Greijdanus's futuristic interpretation and his determination to stay away from Chiliastic speculation, with which he was familiar through the church fathers, he chose for an exegesis of Revelation 11:8 that ultimately denied the covenant identity of the city referred to.

What does Melito do with Revelation 11:8? Listen to what he says in his Easter homily:

> There has been a new murder in the middle of Jerusalem,
> in the city of the law,
> in the city of the Hebrews,
> in the city of the prophets,
> in the city that is called righteous (PP, 94).

Immediately after this passage, Melito uses the term *plateia*, which is also used in Revelation 11:8. In this homily he quotes from Revelation; Eusebius even reports that Melito wrote a book on Revelation. Therefore we may take it that he was well acquainted with Revelation, and that it was under the influence of Revelation 11:8 that he spoke of the murder of Christ in the city of the Hebrews, the city of the covenant. The Righteous One was murdered in the middle of the city and the *plateia*, in plain view of all.

The fact that Melito relied on Revelation 11:8 to speak of Jerusalem in such a way indicates that he did indeed apply this text to Jerusalem. I might add that this pastor who made so many statements about the Lamb's confrontation with the synagogue was influenced in this regard by the book of Revelation. For him it was a foregone conclusion that Christians had to oppose the synagogue of satan continually.

Further investigation of Melito's Easter homily and related literature directed against the Jews will contribute more evidence that Revelation was *not* directed against Rome. John's Apocalypse does not admit of a universalizing exegesis in which it is presupposed that the book is addressed to humanity in general. Revelation, like the rest of the New Testament, contains a running polemic against the Jews and their rejection of Christ. It shares this theme with many of the early Christian passion homilies, which were testimonies against the Jews.

The thesis that Revelation is directed against Rome is indefensible on scholarly grounds. It can only be upheld through some sort of allegorizing and demythologizing of the Old Testament and the Jewish motifs it contains, a procedure that strips them of their covenant meaning and pours a universal content into them. This dangerous thesis also has the effect of isolating the book of Revelation from the rest of the New Testament and from the Quartodeciman literature and its early polemics against the Jews.

Fear God and honor the king

In an article entitled "The Relation between Church and State: A Reinterpretation," Kurt Aland has argued that the generally accepted view is in need of correction (see *Journal of Theological Studies*, XIX, 1968, pp. 115-27). Our view of the early church's attitude toward authority is wrong, he claims. The church did not take an antithetical stance toward the Roman empire: in fact, the Christian leaders took a *positive* attitude toward Roman rule, an attitude that did not begin with Constantine the Great and his acceptance of the Christian faith.

Aland goes on to argue that the book of Revelation is an exception to this pattern in that it speaks of Rome as "Babylon." Thus he accepts the view that Revelation follows in the footsteps of Jewish apocalyptic literature in its nationalistic rejection of Rome. Other scholars have also reached the conclusion that the book of Revelation breaks with the rest of early Christianity in its attitude to government authority. There are special influences evident in this book, which are intended for only a small circle. The influence of the enemies of the state is part of the reason why the book of Revelation was resisted so strongly before it was accepted as part of the canon—or so the argument runs.

Ignoring these comments on the book of Revelation for the moment, we should focus on the fact that recent studies do indeed indicate that neither early Christianity nor the New Testament itself took a hostile attitude toward the Roman authorities (see Rom. 13:1-7; Titus 3:1; I Pet. 2:13-17; I Tim. 2:2). The testimony is overwhelming.

At the end of the first century, the church of Rome wrote a letter to the church of Corinth. In a prayer at the end of this letter we find the following words:

> Thou, Master, hast given the power of sovereignty to them through thy excellent and inexpressible might, that we may know the glory and honor given to them by thee, and be subject to them, in nothing resisting thy will. And to them, Lord, grant health, peace, concord, firmness, that they may administer the government which thou hast given them without offense (translation by K. Lake).

In this prayer we sense nothing of the Zealot's hatred of the

beast Rome—even though the prayer comes from the city
of Rome itself.

In an apologia addressed to the emperor, Melito of Sardis spoke of the possibility of peaceful coexistence between
"church" and "state." Men like Tertullian and Cyprian
appealed for prayers on behalf of the authorities. They
were well aware that the disappearance of Roman authority
would lead to anarchy, and they expressed this openly.

The late date generally assigned to the book of
Revelation goes back to Irenaeus. It is then argued that
Revelation is a protest against Rome. Yet Irenaeus himself
was grateful for the Romans. The Romans, he declared,
had given the world peace and had taken the danger out of
travel from country to country (see *Adversus haereses*, IV,
30-1).

The plot thickens, for later Augustine did indeed compare Rome with Babylon (see *The City of God*, XVIII,
23). But that's all he did—compare them. He did not
equate them. And we must bear in mind that a lot of water
had gone over the dam by then. There had been Christian
emperors in the west, but their rule was a disappointment
in many respects. There may have been Donatist influences
on Augustine, and the nature/grace scheme certainly
played a role in his thought. (Think of the earthly city and
the heavenly city.) Ideas that rose in Augustine's mind at a
fairly advanced point in Christian history should not be
projected back onto earlier writers. Aland is right in calling
for a reinterpretation.

We must also break with the view that the book of
Revelation represents an isolated attitude, that it represents
the thinking of only a small group or was intended for a
small circle. Revelation is not a discordant ending added to
the New Testament by a nationalistic Zealot.

Some scholars have pointed to Jewish writings that apply
the name *Babylon* to Rome in typological fashion (see II
Baruch 11:1; 67:78; Sibylline Oracles, V, 162-77). Now,
this does not by any means prove that the name *Babylon*
always refers to Rome, nor does it prove that the Christians

thought the same way. The identification of "Babylon" with Rome in I Peter 5:13 is highly dubious. There is no good reason for accepting this text as star witness in favor of the thesis "Babylon = Rome."

We must also remember that there are occasions when the Sibylline Oracles speak of Babylon and actually mean Babylon—not Rome. Sometimes scholars play games with such alleged evidence. Moreover, the fact that the Sibylline Oracles call *Jerusalem* the "great city" (V, 154, 226, 413) is often ignored, while the reference to the Jews as people of the land of sodomy is also relevant to Revelation 11:8 (see VI, 21). If we consider this evidence carefully and do our best to soften our resistance to change, we see that it is indeed time to consider a reinterpretation.

Strange things happen in history. Today a stream of potent arguments is not enough to convince advocates of covenant Christian living that the covenant is also the alpha and omega of the book of Revelation. These advocates of covenant living are subservient to authority and want nothing to do with revolution. But at various points they capitulate to the theology of revolution, which seeks to show that the Bible is not always opposed to revolution. According to this new theology, there is a plurality of political outlooks present within the New Testament: Romans 13:1-7 and the book of Revelation represent the two extremes.

In orthodox circles, the thesis is watered down somewhat: the opposed political viewpoints become "differences in nuance." Yet such defenders of orthodoxy are ultimately defenseless in the face of the theology of revolution, for they have already yielded on the basic point, namely, the *political* interpretation of the book of Revelation.

False exegesis ultimately condemns itself. Hence the problem of how to read the book of Revelation and dispose of antiquated views for which there is no basis is no mere academic question. Finally, let's not forget that proper exegesis and understanding of the Scriptures leads to blessings.

The Book of Revelation in Covenant Context

The visions and the seven messages

The seven "letters" are the best known and most discussed part of the book of Revelation. But how do these messages fit in with the rest of the book? There are some scholars who argue that they were added later.

I don't accept that conclusion. The seven messages are an integral part of the book; they are solidly rooted in the book's main purpose. The way Christ is referred to in each of the messages points back to the description of Him in chapter 1. The promise at the end of each message is bound up with the later visions. Within the messages we come across motifs that appear in the visions—white garments, impure food, satan, and so forth.

Let's assume that the book of Revelation is indeed a unified whole and raise the question that needs to be asked: What is the relationship between the seven messages and the rest of the book? The usual answer is that there is only a loose connection. The visions are directed against emperor worship, but this is not yet obvious from the messages. Once we cease identifying the visions as a protest against emperor worship, however, our eyes are opened to the covenant language spoken in both the messages and the visions.

The form of the messages reminds us of an ancient Near Eastern covenant and even presupposes the structure of a Biblical covenant. That structure includes a redemptive historical prologue, covenant stipulations, and covenant threats. In the visions, the emphasis falls on the covenant *threats*. The covenant curses of Leviticus 26 are worked out dramatically. The judgment on an apostate city is sketched in colors that remind us of the judgment of Sodom and Egypt.

There is an even clearer connection to be noted. In the messages the common theme is faithfulness to the received confession in the face of the synagogue of satan. The synagogue of satan is mentioned explicitly in the messages to Smyrna and Philadelphia, and in the other messages it forms the background of the admonition. The churches had grown weak in their confession. In connection with Pergamum and Thyatira, there is even talk of "immorality" or "adultery." This charge must be read in Old Testament terms and applied to the relationship to the synagogue. The Christians in those two churches were inclined to compromise. Therefore they faced the punishment of which Hebrews warned (12:17; 10:39).

The visions underscore the threat of punishment. Choosing for the Lamb means saying goodbye to the synagogue. Jesus's words about Jerusalem would be fulfilled. The grim trio of hunger, the sword and pestilence would ride out against the temple city. The Old Testament prophecies would be fulfilled again in the New Testament days.

Typical Jewish motifs appear in the visions—a lampstand, palm branches, a trumpet. The language used echoes the Old Testament more than any other New Testament book. We are reminded of the covenant by words, symbols and themes. Jesus Christ takes away the privileged position of the synagogues and gives it to the churches, but not in a matter-of-fact way. He adds a warning: see to it that the same thing doesn't happen to you!

Where does Revelation 11 fit in?

The usual way to divide the visions is: (1) chapters 4-11, (2) chapters 12-22. Is this a proper division?

I believe that this division will not further insight into the central message of the book of Revelation, for it keeps us from seeing the role that the "great city" of Revelation 11 plays in the rest of the book. Revelation 11 winds up on an island by itself as a Jewish pamphlet within a book directed against Rome. How, then, is it to be interpreted?

Capable interpreters who keep the Jewish context and the struggle against the synagogue in mind as they read the other New Testament books and who have an ear for covenant language are often led astray by the mistaken assumption that Revelation is a relatively late book and also by the curious division of the book that is now widely accepted. Therefore they approach Revelation differently. The fruitful interpretive methods that they apply elsewhere they do not apply to the book of Revelation. As a result, they wind up repeating the usual political-cultural exegesis.

Fortunately, there is another division possible, a division that seems obvious enough once it is explained. In chapter 10 we find a new vision in which John is called. If a division is to be made, that's the place for it.

In chapter 11 we come across two themes that are later worked out at length: (1) the beast and (2) the great city. Chapter 12 shows us the "father" of the beast, and chapter 13 introduces us to his demonic companion, who is behind the work of the false prophets. False prophecy is what Scripture itself calls it, and it is a phenomenon that can occur also in a covenant context.

In chapters 14 and 16, the city that will be dealt with in later chapters is already mentioned. The judgment on that city by way of the demonic trio is sketched.

Thus chapter 11 is not insular in character. What we are first shown in chapters 4-9 is worked out from chapter 11 on. In chapter 11 we get a summary and survey of the themes that are unfolded in the chapters to come. What chapter 12 begins to talk about, then, is not a brand-new subject. There is continuity throughout the book of Revelation.

Revelation is not a carelessly composed book that deals

with Rome for a while, then Jerusalem, then some other world city, and takes up a series of entirely different topics in the "letters." Revelation is a unified, carefully composed book that speaks covenant language throughout and points constantly to Jesus Christ, the Lamb. Christ has come with grace for His people who follow Him. He "passes over" them, but He will not "pass over" those who are unfaithful to the covenant. Woe to you, Jerusalem! Wake up, sleeping church! Hear, O Israel! The hour of judgment is near!

If Revelation is divided the wrong way, we will not understand the book properly. Change is in order if we are to recognize the covenant framework.

What do I get out of it?

This question is bound to come up when people are told that the prophecies of judgment in the book of Revelation point to a destruction of Jerusalem, which took place almost 2000 years ago. People argue that in that case the book of Revelation has no message for today's church. It doesn't speak to *us*.

Perhaps we could respond to this question with another question: What did the first readers of the book of Revelation get out of those prophecies if they concerned an antichrist in a vague, distant, faraway "end time"? Couldn't they argue that the book had no message for them?

"Surely I am coming soon," says Jesus at the end of the book. How can that assurance be reconciled with the passage of nineteen centuries since then? Defenders of the futuristic interpretation have had to perform exegetical acrobatics to get around that problem.

But that's not all there is to be said in response. We could point to the Old Testament as well, where we also read about imminent judgments, judgments that have since come and gone. Does the church of the new covenant get

nothing out of such passages? Are they without a message
for us? Are they recorded in our Bibles only to supply us
with sensationalistic illustrations to use in sermons about
events in the world today?

Don't these Old Testament prophecies show us *how* the
God of the covenant deals with His people? And doesn't
that speak to today's church, which lives in covenant with
the same God? God remains the same through all ages.
Today's church also faces the kindness and severity of God
(Rom. 11:17-22).

When we are confronted with a prophecy from the New
Testament, are we supposed to suddenly apply different
hermeneutical norms? Should we begin with egoistic con-
siderations, asking what's in it for us? Or should we admit
that we're on the wrong track when we begin with such a
question?

People have always been interested in manmade
apocalypticism. Today there is modern apocalypticism in a
variety of forms, e.g. the gruesome predictions about the
imminent destruction of the world through atom bombs.
Such apocalypticism has little to do with the gospel; the
resemblance is purely superficial.

Phrases are borrowed from the book of Revelation and
torn out of their covenant context, their reference to the
church, God's covenant people. Covenant judgment is
turned into secularized ruin and wrath. No one is surprised to
hear Churchill talking about the "vials of wrath" or to see
Leon Uris borrowing the name *Armageddon* for his book
about the cold war in Berlin. Apocalyptic language is common property; it is part of our culture. Christians who are
looking for popularity join in the game. Success is assured,
for everyone loves a good scare. This is part of the reason
for the Hal Lindsey phenomenon.

What we must remember is that our reading of Scripture
may never be determined by what we find amusing or
edifying. The question we must ask ourselves is what the
book of Revelation says within the framework of Scripture
as a whole. The real issue at stake is the glory of God.

The Word of God as it comes to us in John's Apocalypse warns us that judgment begins with the house of God. When we look at our bourgeois, middle-class churches with their complacency and self-satisfaction, doesn't this message make us feel uncomfortable?

The book of Revelation is not a "Handbook to the Future" or a political almanac; it is a message to the church from its Head and King. The King is telling the church to hold on to what He has given her. Translating that message for today's situation, we would say: "In these days of revolutionary Christianity divorced from any confession, we must be doubly sure to hold fast our confession. If the church becomes a false church, she turns into a synagogue of satan. Then the same God who has so often entered covenant history with judgment will make His presence felt once more. Using the sword of His mouth, He will strike the church with covenant wrath."

That's the message of the book of Revelation. Be sure not to weaken when the church's confession is attacked and undermined. In Revelation all the Old Testament prophecies come together as prophecies of Jesus Christ. Anyone who reads through the Revelation to John in search of cultural philosophy or fortune-telling has not understood what the Spirit says to the churches.

There is a twisted mentality behind the complaint that there's nothing in Revelation for *me* if its prophecies refer to the destruction of Jerusalem. Most of the other Bible books do not leave much room for the yearning for apocalypticism, which is in essence pagan. Therefore people seize on the book of Revelation as a platform on which to build their wild fantasies about the future.

It may sound harsh, but in essence this yearning for apocalypticism is a love of false prophecy, of prophecy rooted in man's own heart and mind and will. We may never allow our needs and desires to dictate our interpretation of the book of Revelation. Revelation is God's Word for the *churches*. That's the framework we must use in our reading of the last book of the Bible. It is a covenant book appealing to us to be faithful to the covenant. At bottom it is no "different" than the other Bible books. It speaks the same covenantal language. We may not water that language down by seeking political and cultural fulfillments for its prophecies. The book of Revelation is not to be neutralized or tampered with in any way:

> I warn every one who hears the words of the prophecy in this book: if any one adds to them, God will add to him the plagues described in this book, and if any one takes away from the words of the book of this prophecy, God will take away his share of the tree of life and of the holy city, which are described in this book (Rev. 22:18-19).

Are we ready to listen to the pure language of the Revelation to John and let the book itself tell us what the message is?

The proof of the pudding

Focusing on Revelation 17 and 18 as a source of examples, I would now like to show you how this covenantal interpretation of the book of Revelation works out in practice. After all, the proof of the pudding is in the eating.

Why these two chapters? Because the defenders of the political interpretation are so sure that the "great city" as it appears here is "Rome."

In Jeremiah 4:30-1 we read:

> And you, O *desolate* one,
> what do you mean that you *dress in scarlet*,
> that you deck yourself with *ornaments of gold*,
> that you enlarge your eyes with paint?
> In vain you beautify yourself.
> Your lovers despise you;
> they seek your life.
> For I heard a cry as of a woman in travail,
> anguish as of one bringing forth her first child,
> the cry of the daughter of Zion gasping for breath,

stretching out her hands,
"*Woe* is me! I am fainting before murderers."

There is some dispute about the translation of these verses. Many newer translations leave out the *desolate*, for it does not appear in the Septuagint. This word appears in the Hebrew text as a masculine form, but it fits in well with the emancipated figure of Judah, the daughter of Zion.

We must not assume that Baruch, Jeremiah's secretary, didn't have his mind on his work when he recorded these words. Nor should we assume that the word *desolate* is intended to make us think of Judah as a victim who seeks to charm her conquerors with her ornaments and dress. No, Jeremiah is pointing ahead to the judgment that will strike Judah, a judgment he already sketched earlier.

The same Hebrew verb behind the word *desolate* was used earlier in the chapter: "The whole land is laid waste" (vs. 20). In visionary style, verse 23 sketches the future as though it were already present: "I looked on the earth, and lo, it was waste and void; and to the heavens, and they had no light."

That's the kind of language Jeremiah addresses to Judah in verse 30: "You are laid waste. You are waste and void, no matter how much you may beautify yourself." Verse 31 works this out further: Jeremiah already hears cries of woe from the daughter of Zion as she perishes at the hands of murderers.

If we simply let Jeremiah 4:30-1 stand and resist the urge to correct it and improve on it, our ears are opened to echoes of it in Revelation 17. The harlot is "arrayed in purple and scarlet, and bedecked with gold and jewels and pearls" (vs. 4). The similarity is no coincidence, nor is it limited to words and sounds. Neither is *Rome* being sketched in colors first used to depict apostate Judah. The song sung in Revelation is not a song of the covenant adapted for use against the wicked "world."

The echoes of Jeremiah 4:30 in Revelation 17 are by no means isolated and insignificant. Jeremiah had pointed to

repeated instances of unfaithfulness to Yahweh on the part
of Judah. The love and devotion of the young bride (Jer.
2:2) has been replaced by devotion to worthless idols (vs. 5).
Judah's lust for apostasy is sketched in stark, realistic terms
in verses 23-4. Judah has given herself to another man
(3:1); she has "played the harlot with many lovers."

Judah deserves to be called the "faithless one." When we
consider the fact that the prophets repeatedly speak of for-
saking the covenant as harlotry and adultery (Is. 1:21;
Ezek. 16:22; Hos. 1-3), the pattern in Revelation falls into
place. Revelation 17 carries on the line of Jeremiah 4:30 by
speaking within the framework of the covenant. Thus the
subject is not "Rome" but "Judah."

It is striking that Revelation 17:16 is also reminiscent of
Jeremiah 4:30. Here we read that the ten horns will hate
the harlot and make her "desolate." The word *desolate* in
this verse is the same word that we find in Matthew 23:38,
according to a great number of early manuscripts. This
word *desolate* appears to be in disfavor among many com-
mentators, even though it also points back to Jeremiah (see
22:5; 12:7). There almost seems to be a conspiracy against
this word!

In Revelation 17:16 we read that judgment is carried out
on the harlot. The woman is made desolate and naked.
(Compare Ezekiel 16:37ff; 23:45ff; and Hosea 2:2, 9, which
are all texts directed at the covenant people.) This Jezebel,
who gets dolled up (see II Kings 9:30—eyes painted, head
adorned), is struck by the judgment of Jeremiah 4:30,
where we also read about painted eyes, ornaments of gold,
and scarlet clothes.

Jezebel is mentioned in Revelation 2:20 and is referred to
again in 19:2. In II Kings 9:7 we read that a young prophet
anointed Jehu and commissioned him to strike down the
house of his master Ahab "that I may avenge the blood of
my servants the prophets, and the blood of all the servants
of the LORD at the hand of Jezebel" (KJV). The Revised
Standard Version leaves out the reference to the *hand* of
Jezebel: "that I may avenge on Jezebel . . . ." It also leaves

out this reference in Revelation 19:2, where the King James Version reads: ". . .and hath avenged the blood of his servants at her hand."

Jezebel, apparently, was the model for the descriptions in Jeremiah 4:30 and Revelation 17-18: "In her heart she says, 'As queen I sit' " (18:7). We find another reference to the prophets as the Lord's servants in Revelation 11:18 (see also Dan. 9:6, 10).

The more we study these connections and interrelations, the more things come together. Revelation 17 and 18 are not talking about a heathen city or empire; they are talking about Israel, the covenant people who killed the prophets (I Kings 19:10, 14; Lam. 4:13).

Jesus Christ spoke the same language to the rabbis in Matthew 23:29ff, calling them "sons of those who murdered the prophets" (vs. 31). "Fill up, then, the measure of your fathers . . . that upon you may come all the righteous blood shed on earth" (vs. 32, 35). The "earth" referred to can better read as a reference to the land of the covenant people.

The same theme appears at the end of Revelation 18: "In her was found the blood of prophets and of saints, and of all who have been slain on earth" (vs. 24). Is there any reason to doubt that this blood of prophets and saints was shed by the covenant people? Didn't Jesus Himself point out that no prophet dies outside Jerusalem? (Luke 13:33).

Yet, interpreters insist on reading Revelation 18:24 apart from the Old Testament and the words of Jesus recorded in the "gospels." We are told that the killing of prophets and saints is a reference to what Rome or some anti-Christian world power will do.

L. A. Vos has pointed out that there are words of Jesus behind certain passages in the book of Revelation, and that these words can help us with the interpretation of Revelation (*The Synoptic Traditions in the Apocalypse*, published in 1965, p. 225). This is hardly a reason for surprise, for the Apocalypse is a "revelation of Jesus Christ," a revelation in which more of His words are recorded. We hear echoes of Matthew 23-24 in the book of Revelation.

When Vos turns his attention to the interpretation of Revelation 18:24, he argues that what Jesus said about *Jerusalem* is applied by John to the destruction of *Rome*, the great city of his day. He admits openly that it is not easy to determine why John here alludes to the words of Jesus. Perhaps the sayings of Jesus were so familiar that John thought nothing of using them in a different context.

What we see here is an example of exegetical poverty. For want of a better perspective, it is assumed that some "apocalyptic" figure wrote the book of Revelation using material from many sources. Such are the assumptions demanded by the political interpretation.

The words of Jesus are separated from John's own purpose in writing. John apparently used the form of Jesus' words in talking about an entirely different subject. Thus the resemblances between the prophecies of Jesus and the prophecies recorded in Revelation are merely superficial; they are resemblances in sound and language, not in meaning.

This approach to Revelation obscures and ultimately destroys the unity of the Scriptures. "Why John in such cases alludes to the sayings of Jesus is difficult to determine," writes Vos. Form and content are separated: the message of Revelation is not to be confused with what we read in Matthew 23:35 and the Old Testament prophets.

Once we embark on this path, we are eventually forced to conclude that Revelation is a most unusual Bible book, a book that cannot be approached in the usual way, a book that is not to be interpreted in the light of the rest of Scripture. Not even Jesus' own words shed light on this "revelation of Jesus Christ"!

On the other hand, we should be thankful that Vos points out the connection between Revelation 18:24 and Matthew 23:35, even if the connection is only a formal resemblance for him. The three books that Greijdanus wrote about Revelation make no mention whatsoever of this connection.

It seems to me that if this connection is taken seriously, it will be seen as undermining the political interpretation of the book of Revelation. The eagerness to maintain the political interpretation leads to a false contrast between "Jesus" and "John." The Reformation principle that Scripture is its own interpreter is abandoned, and we remain mired in form criticism.

But if we take a different approach, we get different results. When we approach the Bible in faith as a unified revelation in which the covenant is a dominant theme from beginning to end, we cannot help but conclude that the current exegesis of the book of Revelation is off the mark.

The hermeneutical key that will open up new perspectives and insights is the realization that the book of Revelation follows in the tradition of Christ, the prophets and the apostles by speaking out against "Jerusalem" and covenant apostasy.

The proof of the pudding is in the eating. This we have seen in connection with Revelation 17-18. Many more examples could be given to show that there is a better way of interpreting the book of Revelation. It may frighten us to think that a contemporary application of Revelation involves pointing a finger at the unfaithful church rather than the "wicked world," but such fear should not be allowed to play a role in our exegesis. We must begin by bowing before the Word.

Not an unusual Bible book

The 1930s were tense years in the Netherlands. War clouds were gathering over Europe. In those days of crisis, Prime Minister Hendrik Colijn spoke to the nation on the radio and said: "Don't do anything unusual. Then life will go on as usual."

Colijn turned out to be wrong, for the Netherlands was dragged into the war against its will. But we could well apply his advice to our reading of the book of Revelation. Why not treat it as an ordinary Bible book instead of regard-

ing it as a source of strange and bizarre predictions? Why
create problems where none need exist? Why ask questions
of Revelation that we do not ask of any other Bible book?

We so often stare at this supposedly unusual book with
earnest looks on our faces. We think we see an exegetical
problem in almost every text. Solving those problems, we
assume, requires the imagination and mental agility of a
champion chess player. Applying our ingenuity to the book
of Revelation has almost become a game, a game without a
time limit. Preachers lead the way. No one thinks it strange
when a preacher solemnly declares: "As for this tricky text,
congregation, it seems to me that we are to apply it to . . . ."

In our day of apocalyptic journalism, such bombast is
still in style. The general weariness and frustration that
eventually results from exegetical acrobatics should not
surprise us. We have only ourselves to blame if we let others
do the thinking for us.

Sobriety and levelheadedness are what we need when we
read the Revelation to John. We should read it just as we
read any other Bible book and stop looking for political
predictions about the future. What Revelation gives us in
words and images is a message about the God of the
covenant, the God of all ages. The Easter gospel comes
through in this book, which reminds us how the Lamb has
arisen from among the dead. Christ is on His way with
Messianic blessings—and also Messianic wrath.

The more we approach Revelation in the usual way, the
less mysterious it will seem and the better the message will
come through. When it is read in the context of Scripture as
a whole, it is an open book, a book that speaks to believers
today as they struggle to learn the meaning and value of
their baptism. That's why it's so important to banish all the
false interpretations and misleading applications to Roman
emperors and future political events. Jesus Christ, our
highest Prophet and Teacher, presents a prophetic message
in a situation in Asia Minor in which many of the churches
are threatening to break away from the faith and return to
the synagogue.

Jesus shows us how the Lord finally dismisses Jerusalem, the city that slaughtered the Lamb. Henceforth He will no longer recognize the Jews as His people.

Isn't this message relevant to our time, when there are so many who want to be religious while refusing to accept the true gospel? The book of Revelation speaks to our ecumenical age with its false peace offensives and warns us not to seek détente in the struggle against the false gospel. What fellowship can there be between wheat and chaff, light and darkness?

Revelation is by no means a mysterious book. In its redemptive historical prologue about a kingdom of priests, we have the foundation for its covenant stipulations. Hear, O Israel. He who has an ear . . . .

The people who were led out of bondage through Jesus Christ are now warned against returning to the house of bondage. If they go back they will be subject to the plagues that struck Egypt. The Apocalypse is not a movie showing us a global apocalyptic ending to history. No, it is a book of comfort and admonition addressed to the church as it goes about its work in the world, a book rich in prophetic language and symbols.

Perhaps the most unusual thing about Revelation is that it's an ordinary Bible book. May the challenge of Hal Lindsey and the confusion about the book of Revelation open our eyes again to the message Jesus preaches at the end of the Bible, namely, that our covenant God remains the same in His grace and in His wrath. He is the God "who is and who was and who is to come" (Rev. 1:4).